Gelato with the Pope:

and other adventures
of a travel writer
in Europe

The stanza of poetry used is by William Wordsworth,
(1802) *Strange Fits of Passion Have I Known.*

Also by Kim Herdman

Selected poems from
Do Whales Jump at Night?
Poems For Kids
edited by Florence McNeil

Gelato with the Pope

and other adventures
of a travel writer
in Europe

KIM HERDMAN

Bamberry Cove Books Vancouver

1 3 5 7 9 10 8 6 4 2

Canadian Cataloguing in Publication Data

Herdman, Kim, 1962

Gelato with the Pope
ISBN 0-9698704-0-X
1.Herdman, Kim, 1962-- Journeys--Europe. 2. Travelers--Europe--Anecdotes. 3. Europe--Description and travel.
I. Title.

D923.H47 1997 914.04'559 C97-910727-X

Bamberry Cove Books
Vancouver, British Columbia
(604) 241-4194

Distributed by:
Sandhill Book Marketing Ltd.
#99-1270 Ellis Street (rear)
Kelowna, British Columbia V1Y 1Z4
To order: 1-800-667-3848

Front cover artwork by Kim Herdman
Back cover photograph by Kim Herdman
Cover design by Anne Dunnett and Kim Herdman
Edited by Susan Kernaghan
Production coordinated by Heidi LeRossignol of Behind the Book Production Services

Printed and bound in Canada by Webcom

For my father, Tom, and Stuart -

the three men whose love helped me make it here

Preface

All of the events in this book did happen. I spent a large part of 1991 travelling throughout Europe writing my syndicated column, "Traveller's Notebook", for newspapers throughout North America. However, due to the inherent difficulties of transposing life into text, time has been pruned, telescoped and, in some cases, downright chopped. I have also changed the names of some individuals - such as the retired army officer in "Hitching on Skye" - to protect their privacy. Most of the others you will meet on these pages retain their own names, and I must take this opportunity to apologize to them in advance for any inconsistencies that may have occurred in my memories of events. I have tried my best to record the truth of my encounters with these people, many of whom showed me great kindness during my journey.

Kim Herdman

Acknowledgements

There are many people who helped me bring this book to fruition. The advice and assistance of Nancy Wise, my distributor at Sandhill Book Marketing Ltd., and Heidi LeRossignol, my production coordinator from Behind the Book Production Services, were invaluable. This book would probably not have been published without them. My mother provided me with the much needed financial support. (Thanks, Mom, the cheque is in the mail!) Arlene Berg and Tom Kraft were great proof-readers and all-around cheerleaders throughout the initial writing process.

For all the newspapers and editors who believed in me and printed the travel column this book is based on - thank you. A nod must also go to Rick Steves, whose book Europe through the Back Door (JMP Travel), was an excellent pre-trip guide.

My final thanks are reserved for Stuart Shapiro. Without his love, support and prodding, you would not be reading this now.

Contents

The Continent

United Kingdom and Ireland

i trooping the colour ❖❖❖❖❖❖❖❖

Rose Hughes, my contact at the British Tourist Authority, had told me to be at the Horse Guards by nine thirty. I looked at my watch as the Northern Line tube train zipped me past Charing Cross toward St. James's. It was already nine fifteen.

Rose would not be amused.

I had arrived on her doorstep at the British Tourist Authority a few days before, fresh from Heathrow Airport and spinning my tale about writing a weekly column on Europe for Canadians. She had listened patiently while I explained that, since I was in London, I was hoping to get a pass in to see that symbol of British pomp and circumstance, the Trooping of the Colour.

Rose sipped at a cup of tea and appeared to assess the validity of my credentials. Age: 28. Sex: Female. Height: 5' 8". Weight: State secret. Fact: Syndicated columnist for several well respected newspapers in Canada. Starting on five-month trek across Great Britain and Europe, attempting to uncover the heart of a continent; to see what life was really like in '90's Europe.

With a sigh and a further slurp of her lapsang-souchong, Rose decided to turn a diplomatic blind eye to my Reeboks, knapsack, and general air of scruffiness. She said that she would do what she could to help me. The real Trooping of the Colour had been booked up by dignitaries and primo journalists months in advance but she would try and get me into the rehearsal, with a major general reviewing the troops in place of the queen. Three days and a security check later, I had my blue duty pass in hand.

My adventure was about to begin.

My watch read nine thirty by the time I arrived at the St. James's Park tube station. I bolted up the steps and headed in the direction of the park at a gallop, the minutes ticking away. I was surprised at the number of other people also headed in the direction of the park, most of them in formal military dress. I, in my jeans and sweater, had been expecting a casual event, the blue duty pass in my pocket nothing more than a formality. After all, this was only a rehearsal. The real thing, with royalty and all, was still several weeks away.

I turned the corner onto the Mall and saw that the green expanse of the park was fenced off, soldiers with police dogs dotting the grassy areas normally used by lovers and old age pensioners. A long queue of people stretched along the sidewalk leading to the Horse Guards entrance. Olive-fatigued soldiers and bobbies topped with shiny black helmets were arranged evenly along the Mall.

I flagged down a passing bobby. "Is this the queue to get in to see the Trooping of the Colour?"

There was a cursory glance at my clothing. "May I see your pass, ma'am?"

I flashed him my proud blue ticket.

"Yes, ma'am. This queue here, please."

The queue was already packed with elderly veterans, medals sagging the shoulders of their green serge suits, their wives festooned with hats that would have made the Queen Mum proud. Soldiers in full military kit also waited stolidly in the line, backs straight, buttocks tight.

The security to get in was thorough and unexpected. I had to undergo a quick body search and then a pass through the metal detector before a female police officer opened my bag and probed her way through my tampons looking for plastique.

By the time I finally got in, the stands were already half full. Sandhurst cadets clustered in one area, retired soldiers in another. I hovered at the bottom, watched with a certain amount of disdain by both camps.

Rose had said that the press seats were at the back so I headed up the stairs. Most of these seats were already filled, but not by people in the media. I got a particularly frosty reception from one party of veterans when I implied that they worked for the newspapers. In London, where journalism is tainted by such publications as the *News of the World*, this could be, and was, taken as an insult.

Further back from the so-called media seats, there were raised platforms for the television cameras and commentators. Spotting a group of men in the BBC booth, I decided to climb up in search of directions. Not only did I need to find my seat, but I sensed a growing urgency that I was going to need to find a toilet pretty soon, too.

It was my greatest fear about travelling alone through Europe. Not: "A woman travelling alone is going to be robbed and raped": "You'll be so lonely!", but rather : "How on earth am I going to find a toilet when I really need one!".

The BBC booth was small and the three men inside intent on their discussion. They looked like businessmen, clad as they were in identical grey trenchcoats. Their heads jerked up as I entered, a look of surprise spreading across their bland, middle-aged faces.

"Hi!" I blurted out.

"Hello." They examined me as if I had recently arrived from Pluto. I stepped further into the room. They shrank back an equal distance. I was beginning to get the feeling I was intruding on something here. "I'm looking for the media seats. Do you know where they are?"

Three heads made another up and down examination of my wardrobe. "You're with the press?"

"Yes."

A small smile. "This is television."

"The BBC," one of the other men corrected.

A nod and smile from all three.

"I'm afraid I don't know where the press are to sit," the first man continued.

I turned to face the third man. He was older than the other two and had been watching me with an air of bemusement. "I also can't find a bathroom anywhere. Do you know where the toilets are?"

The older man blinked. The other two looked as if I had asked them to name their most recent sexual conquest. "I have no idea," he answered.

Feeling more and more like an interloper, I backed my way towards the door. "Well, thanks for the help anyway." I excused myself and climbed back down into the stands.

Giving up the fight, I wedged myself into a seat. I didn't care whether it was the press section or not. I had a more important problem to deal with, namely finding the nearest toilet. Rose had told me to be at the rehearsal two hours in advance in order to allow the police to do a thorough security check of the area before the procession started. I still had an hour to wait and then several hours for the trooping ceremony itself. My bladder would never last.

Up again and down the steps at a hop. If nothing else, I was providing entertainment for all the dignitaries sitting patiently in the stands.

"Excuse me. Do you know where the nearest toilet is?" I asked a fur-hatted soldier waiting at the base of the stands.

"Toilets. Hmmm." The gold tassels on his red uniform flapped as he waved his hand to gesture a group of similarly clad soldiers over to us. "Haven't the faintest. Lads!" he shouted, "Do you know where the toilets are?"

With a grimace, I glanced up at the stands. The Sandhurst cadets were leaning forward to get a better vantage point on our conversation.

Four soldiers shook their busbied heads. One pointed his finger in the direction of a bobby on guard on the Mall. "Best ask him."

Upon hearing my question, the bobby pointed across the Mall. I could see a small building through the aluminum security gates and rows of wire fencing. This was, it appeared, the loo.

"It's in St. James's Park," I said, stating the obvious.

"'Fraid so, Luv." He smiled. It was the smile of a man who can drink ten pints of ale and not have to fight his way through the pub crowds to the urinal.

"How on earth am I going to get there?" My voice was rising.

As if to accentuate the desperateness of my plight, a police officer walked past the park toilet with a vicious looking German shepherd on the end of a lead.

"Can't you wait?" he asked. My first deduction had been correct. This was a twenty-gallon bladder kind of man.

"No, I can't," I stated firmly.

There was silence as we both considered the situation. With a sudden movement, he pushed open the security fence in front of us, leaving a small gap. "Well, you better make a run for it then."

I stood still for a moment, pondering my fate. Stay and burst, or head out into No Man's Land and perhaps die in the attempt. Throwing caution to the winds, I bolted out and into the Mall.

The Mall is a wide cement thoroughfare leading from Buckingham Palace through some of the best neighbourhoods in London. Lined with trees, it appeals to the gracious, refined sensibilities of the English. I had wandered across it on several occasions before, dodging taxis and tour buses to reach the other side.

This time I made it five feet before a loud cry echoed along the street from one of the security posts.

"Oi! Get that woman!"

I heard a scrabbling of feet behind me before several fatigue-clad bodies collided with my own and I found myself face down on the pavement.

"I'm just trying to get to the loo!" I bleated out.

A soldier pulled me out of this scrum and onto my feet as a police inspector stormed up to us. He was tall and thin with a bang of grey hair that moved across his face in angry jerks as he spoke. "What is she doing here?" he asked the soldiers.

"I'm trying to get to the bathroom," I answered for them.

I didn't bother to look over the shoulders of the soldiers to see whether the people in the stands were now watching. I knew that I had moved from a passing oddity to full-blown entertainment.

"You're what?!"

"I'm just trying to get to the toilets."

"The toilet!" I felt like an errant schoolgirl about to get swatted by the headmaster. "Have her searched, and then take her to the toilets. Whatever you do, just GET HER OFF THE STREET!" He turned on his heel and stomped back towards the security post.

A few of the bobbies began to giggle. I handed them my duty pass and allowed myself to be ignominiously searched in the middle of the street. I was not particularly concerned about being publicly shamed or even worried about the fate of the sweet bobby who had so foolishly helped me get there. I just needed someone to take me to the toilet.

A five-minute escorted hike through roped-off St. James's Park, which included a bomb-sniffer search of my bag, and I finally found blessed relief. When I was returned to the stands, the bobby who had replaced my accomplice at the Horse Guards entry gate started to laugh.

"Do you need to see my pass?" I asked in an attempt at professionalism and flashed the blue pass in front of his face.

His shoulders began to shake. "No, that's okay. We know who you are," he snickered.

"Really?"

"Yeah. You're the journalist who needed the loo!"

His shoulders began to roll with laughter as I stalked haughtily past him and into the stands.

The Trooping of the Colour finally began with row after row of glistening horses parading down the Mall. The Household Cavalry lined up, several abreast, while tens of busby-topped soldiers marched into the square in front of the Horse Guards and lined up in formation to await their review by the major general.

"What's it like performing before the queen?" I asked a Coldstream Guards retiree sitting in the stands.

He mulled this over for a minute. "Nerve-wracking."

A middle-aged man and his young son sat on my other side. "That's the major general down there," he informed me, upon finding me a neophyte to such events. "The empty carriage following him will hold the queen on the actual trooping day."

He told me that his eldest son had performed in the ceremony many times before. When asked where his son was now, he swelled with pride. "He's serving in the Gulf." He pointed to the small tape recorder in his hand. "I'm recording this for him."

I apologized for babbling away.

"Oh no, talk into it, please," he insisted. "I want him to hear it all, everything, as if he were here."

The massed bands piped up into a rousing regimental march as the major general rode by to review the troops. The movements of the soldiers seemed letter perfect to me. Black busbies spun on cue as a hundred leather-booted feet smacked the pavement in unison. Every once in a while, however, the retired guardsmen around me would shudder. "He turned the wrong way again," I heard them mutter as I scanned the die-straight lines of shoulders for the errant one. I never found him, but judging by the number of shudders, he must have been having a particularly bad day.

When the colour, or regimental flag, was paraded past the sovereign, or in this case, the major general, a rustle of bodies rose to their feet, hats doffed in respect. There was a good cross section of the British military in the stands. Young soldiers, trim and crisp in their uniforms; members of the military aristocracy, their protruding stomachs evidence of too much good food and too little field work;

and retired veterans, their suits a bit worn, their faces creased, but still smiling and happy with their memories.

"It was nice talking to you," I said to the father when the ceremony was over. "And thanks again for all the information."

He beamed over at me. "Oh no. It helped make it interesting for Tim." He clicked off the tape recorder and shifted in his seat to pick up his large carry-all bag. His mouth dropped open at the sight of something and he pointed up into the stands. "Look, James. Look who's up there!"

The boy turned to follow his father's gaze to the television booths.

"Who is it?" I asked. All I could see were the three businessmen climbing down from the BBC platform.

"You don't know?"

I shook my head no. "I haven't the faintest. Those were the three men I was talking to when I was trying to find the loo."

A look of horror passed over the father's face. "You asked him about the loo?" he whispered.

"Him? Which him?"

A finger pointed towards the older man.

"Yes, that's him. That's the man I was speaking to."

His mouth dropped open. "Do you know who that is?"

"No."

James butted in with a name that was unfamiliar to me.

"Who's that?" I asked.

This flummoxed the father for a moment. "He's, well, an institution in Britain. He's like your, umm," he paused and then inspiration struck, "Like your Walter Cronkite."

I started to giggle, my giggles growing into loud, hooting laughter. The father had to slap me on the back a few times as the stands around us slowly emptied and the soldiers trooped off to their assorted homes.

It was certainly a momentous start to a journey.

ii cream teas and cathedrals ❖❖❖❖❖

The Nipper Bus rattled west along the A4. A breath of warm, hay-scented air blew in through the windows to remind me that I had finally left the brownish smog of London behind me.

I was here in the southern countryside to investigate the tradition of the cream tea. When plotting my itinerary back home, there had seemed nothing more quintessentially English than a cream tea. But where to start? How do you pick one from the myriad of choices? There was Sunday afternoon tea at the Ritz, posh and polite, with table after table of blue blooded women wearing flowered silks and large, draping hats. Or the cream teas of Cornwall, known for the rich decadence of their butter yellow creams and thick flaky scones. But I was constantly drawn back to Devon, the original home of the thick, sweet clotted cream that transports an afternoon snack to the epicurean heights of an English cream tea. Killerton House, a beautiful National Trust estate just outside of the Devon capital of Exeter, seemed to perfectly fit the bill.

Green patches of pasture flashed by, interspersed with rich

yellow fields of mustard. Jersey cows grazed happily beside thatched cottages that looked like something recreated from a child's toy village. The warmth of the sun on my cheek reminded me that summer was not far off. When I had called the estate about the interview, the voice over the telephone had informed me that I was to get off at the sign for Broadclyst village and hike up the road to the house itself. They were expecting me early so that I would have time for a tour of the house before tasting their cream tea.

"Excuse me," I turned to the woman seated beside me on the bus. She was sixtyish and delicate as a sparrow, with the kind of white-gloved propriety that makes me feel gauchely North American.

She turned towards me and raised her eyebrows in greeting. "I was wondering if you could tell me when we get to the stop for Killerton House."

Her thin lips lifted in a small smile. "Of course. I happen to be going there myself."

The silver-topped head in front of us turned around and an Aussie voice blurted out with a twang sharp enough to slice cheddar. "Did you say Killerton House?"

"Yes," I said.

"Isn't that something! I'm going there, too. We three can make a party!"

The Englishwoman glanced from the Australian to myself and did everything but wrinkle her nose at the prospect.

We exchanged names and hometowns. The Australian woman was on a tour of gardens in Great Britain and was excited about seeing the large and well respected one at Killerton House. I mentioned only that I was on a trip around Europe, leaving both women to place me squarely in the backpacker brigade. The Englishwoman, whose name was Janet, informed us that she worked as a volunteer at Killerton House several days a week.

The conversation shifted to a discussion of the health of English bedding plants and I turned my attention to the window. Was Janet a widow? Or a married woman of the flower-growing, church-going type? Her manner as she spoke to the Australian was arch and stiff, but I thought I detected a trace of loneliness in her voice.

Our small bus rattled along a country lane towards Broadclyst, stopping every mile or so whenever a woman with a shopping bag over her arm flagged it down. The two women talked on about weed killers and the BBC's *Garden Time* radio show, effectively excluding me from the conversation.

"Here we are." Janet stood up and made the kind of vague waving gesture to the bus driver that an Edwardian lady might have made at an annoying mosquito.

The three of us clambered down out of the bus into a cloud of dust. Immediately the pungent smell of cow manure penetrated my nostrils, reminding me of childhood summers in the country.

With another vague hand signal, Janet guided us across the lane and along a path cut through a grassy field.

"There is Killerton House," she said proudly.

The house rose up on a small hill above us, the landscape around it gently sloping away as if in deference to the occupants of the house. On the left, you could see the ambrosial peaches and blush pinks of the garden, a lone tourist beetling away along its paths, camera at the ready.

The house itself was an angular block of aged stone, coated with white-purple vines of wisteria. The driveway wound up to the front door, and the front lawn - an unbroken expanse of lush green- glimmered in the late spring sun.

"This is the visitor information area," Janet said to me as we arrived at a small building beside the house. She excused herself and headed into the house while the Australian wandered off into the garden.

I nodded my thanks and walked in and introduced myself to the woman who was minding the admissions box. With a flurry of excitement, she pointed me in the direction of the house itself.

The white front door opened with a push and I entered the cool, wood-tinted interior of the entrance area. It was decorated in the style of an eighteenth century country house, with newspapers and stationery sitting on a table as if they were awaiting delivery on a silver salver. A woman sitting at an antique desk jumped to her feet and scurried to my side.

"Hello. Are you the journalist?"

"Yes." I dropped my bag onto the ground and glanced around the room. The walls were hung with portraits of the Acland family. "I have an appointment with Denise for ten o' clock."

"Yes, of course. Have a seat here and I'll tell her you've arrived." She indicated a tapestry-covered chair and waited for me to sit.

"Denise will be here in a moment," she said after a brief phone conversation.

A few minutes later, a tiny young woman appeared in the entrance hall. "Hello, Kim. It's nice to meet you. My name is Denise." A diminutive hand was held out to me. "I'm the administrator here. May I give you a tour of the house?"

The tour started in the music room, a Georgian style room dominated by a large chamber organ. The rose-coloured ceiling was scalloped with white plaster relief. The rest of the room was furnished with heavily embroidered chairs, draped with antimacassars in a wealth of colours.

Killerton House had originally been the home of the Aclands, a family with a long history in Devon. Central to political and royal doings, it was a busy country estate from the 1700's on. Gladstone and Lloyd George were frequent guests here, as were other exponents of the Aclands liberal political beliefs. The estate and house were donated to the National Trust by the late Sir Richard Acland at the end of World War Two.

"And this is the library."

We swept into a room lined with polished wood bookshelves and aging volumes. The style was similar to that of the drawing room, with the walls decorated in intricate plaster cameo work. Large bay windows opened out onto the garden. In one section, turn-of-the-century clothing was displayed.

"And this is Bob," Denise introduced me to a rotund man

bouncing excitedly on his toes beside one of the roped-off exhibitions.

He nodded in a secretive way and winked at me. "I know who you are," he said in the sing song voice that boys use to tease girls in the schoolyard.

"Yes, I was beginning to get that feeling," I laughed. Denise and Bob joined in.

"We don't get many journalists coming here, you see," Denise explained. "It's a bit of an event for our volunteers."

"Yes, we don't get interviewed by 'the press' very often," Bob added.

"I see. Well, I hope I do you justice then."

"I'm sure you will, Miss. I'm sure you will," he called out after us.

Sunlight filtered in a diffused haze through the Edwardian skylights that crowned the stairs. The air smelled cool and damp. It was easy to imagine a parade of uniformed housemaids scurrying behind the closed doors, lighting fires and ironing dresses. At any minute Gladstone might appear in the corridor, muttering to himself with a clutch of speech notes in his hand.

Denise led me upstairs and showed me through the displays of the Killerton costume collection. Then with a push of the door, we entered the master bedroom.

Standing in one corner, three women were huddled in conversation. They turned as we entered, and I noticed Janet among them.

"Kim, I'd like you to meet some more of our volunteers," said Denise as we approached. "Although the grapevine informs me that you've already met one of them. Janet has been telling us all about her adventures with you this morning. It sounds like the two of you became quite good friends."

The two other elderly women twittered with the giggly excitement of teenagers meeting a pop star.

Janet's eyes met mine. Her face was rigid and I could see a desperate vulnerability in her eyes.

"Yes, that's right." I said and saw her shoulders rise and then relax. "We had a lovely chat." Janet silently nodded. "Without Janet, I'd still be on that bus. Probably somewhere around Brighton by now."

The clutch of women giggled and looked at Janet with what seemed like new respect. The sharp contours of her face had softened and I thought I detected some genuine warmth in the small smile she offered me.

"It was nothing," she said softly.

We left them in a huddle, Janet retelling her own embroidered description of our bus trip in from town.

The real purpose of my trip was awaiting me at the end of the tour. Since I had visited England many times before, I already knew that the quality of cream teas could range from glorious to god-awful. As soon as the tourists arrived each summer, signs for cream teas would sprout magically on sidewalks from Margate to Manchester. But this time I wanted to truly experience the real thing: no dry scones or bottled heavy cream for me.

In the small teashop situated in the old pantry of the house, I sat down with Denise and the teashop manager to feast on a real Devon cream tea. First a waitress in the uniform of an Edwardian servant, prim black dress covered with a crisp white linen apron, placed a plate of golden scones in front of me, followed by a steaming pot of tea and an assortment of dishes. I could smell the sweet tang of strawberry jam rising from one of the dishes, while the other held a large dollop of Devon clotted cream. It was yellow and thick, the consistency of softened butter.

"You don't have to eat them all," Denise warned me as I topped a flaky creation with a mixture of jam and thick, clotted cream.

I took a bite from the tottering creation and savoured the contrast in textures between the warm floury scone, the sensuous cream and the slightly tart jam.

Denise and the manager smiled as I gave the universal thumbs up sign of approval.

"Here now, this is the way we eat them in Devon." The teashop manager reached out for my plate.

She first topped a scone with a thick layer of cream and then coated it with strawberry jam. "Always the cream first. Then the jam, always strawberry. That's how you know it's real. That's how you know it's truly Devon."

I nodded and took another bite. It certainly tasted like the real thing to me.

* * *

It was early evening as the train eased into Canterbury, the last stop on my tour of the South. In five days I had bounced across Devon and up through Bath and Wales, before shooting my way back across England to its southeastern tip. I nurtured a fantasy of being hit by a car so that I would be forced to rest in a nice, warm hospital bed. I even imagined the brave telephone call back to my editors in Canada. "I was crossing the street on my way to 10 Downing Street when this fish and chips van came out of nowhere. The doctor says I might lose the use of my legs if I continue on with my columns, but I feel I must. No, no, I must continue. Well, I suppose I could rest here for a few days. That is, if you insist."

My diet wasn't doing me any favours either. I started each day with a calorically-loaded cholesterol feast better known as a cooked breakfast, followed by a lunch and dinner of cheddar cheese sandwiches and pints of lager. I needed a rest, and a leisurely examination of Canterbury Cathedral seemed to fit the bill.

The woman seated behind the visitor information desk at Canterbury Cathedral seemed pleased at my inquiry about an interview with one of the vicars.

"Mabel, who do you think should speak to this young lady?"

A floral frocked woman peered up from a tome she was searching through and examined me with a smile.

"She's a Canadian journalist, writing a story about the life of the cathedral," the woman explained.

Mabel pondered this for a moment. "Canon Brett, I think."

"Of course," the first lady nodded her head in agreement. "Canon Brett is the man for you." I took the pamphlet she held out to me. "Here's a map of the cathedral. Now, first off, I think we should set you up with a tour of the cathedral. Are you free right now?"

I nodded yes.

"Well, our best tour guide is giving a tour in fifteen minutes. Here," she pinned a button on my sweater to show I was part of the group, "I'll walk you over there."

The tour group was clustered around the altar awaiting the arrival of our guide. Bunched in groups of ones and twos, they stood chatting about restaurant prices and snapping the occasional photo. Our guide, when he arrived, turned out to be a rather long-winded academic. I busied myself with studying the cathedral. Its Gothic and Norman architecture soared in a huge central aisle towards the altar. Stunning stained glass, rich with the reds and blues of Chartres, punctuated the pillared walls.

Perhaps the most famous site on the tour was that of the slaying of Thomas à Becket. A simple stone inscribed with his name rests in the floor at the site of his murder. I looked closer as we stopped for a brief discussion of the event. The stone appeared to be stained a faint crimson colour. I looked again. It was definitely tinted in spots with a red haze. I commented on this to our guide.

The group peered more closely at the stone.

"You know, you're right," he answered with a touch of confusion. "It does look a bit discoloured, doesn't it?"

"Yes, but isn't it unusual that it should be that colour. You know, the colour of blood?"

There was silence from the group, and I thought I detected a general outbreak of goosebumps as we moved with quickened footsteps towards the next stop in the tour.

After thoroughly examining the cathedral, I wandered back to check on the progress of my appointment with Canon Brett.

Mabel was now supervising the information desk. "Hello, Dearie. Did you have a nice tour?"

"Yes." I thought it best not to mention the mysterious blood-stained stone. "Do you have a time yet for my interview with Canon Brett tomorrow?"

"Tomorrow?" A frown wrinkled Mabel's ample brow. "I don't think it's tomorrow, Dearie. No, here it is." She picked up a piece of paper and examined the scribbling on it. "Canon Brett has re-arranged his schedule so that he can speak to you today. Isn't that lovely of him?" A 100 watt smile was beamed in my direction at the beneficence of Canon Brett.

"Today?" I sputtered out. "When?"

"Let me see. Four o'clock. That way you can speak to Canon Brett and then the two of you can attend the Evensong service you were enquiring about this morning."

My watch said one forty-five. That left me little more than two hours to prepare for the interview.

"Is that all right, Dearie?" Mabel inquired.

"Yes, fine," I started to back my way out of the office, busily rescheduling my day, when Mabel fluttered a piece of paper out to me.

"Here, Dearie. Can't forget this."

"What is it?"

"Canon Brett's address. You couldn't very well find him without it, could you?"

I scurried up the High Street, regretting that my decision to stay at a youth hostel also entailed a twenty minute hike from the centre of town to get to it. Under one arm I held a plastic Top Shop bag with a hurriedly bought grey skirt in it.

I had stayed in hostels before and found they were a wonderful boost to my budget, cutting my living costs in half. More importantly, they gave me the opportunity to meet people outside of work and cook my own meals, knocking out two of the negatives of travelling: loneliness and bad food.

I burst into the youth hostel and galloped towards the staircase.

"Hello," a small, blonde-headed boy chirruped from his position seated at the bottom of the stairs.

"Hello," I puffed out.

"Why are you running?"

"I'm late for an appointment."

I tried to step around him but he followed me like a faithful spaniel. He looked about five, dressed in patched shorts and a white t-shirt.

"My name is Peter." Obviously he was too young to understand the art of the tactful escape. Even though my feet were moving quickly up the stairs, he was doggedly keeping up.

"That's nice, Peter. My name is Kim, and I'm afraid I'm in a terrible hurry." We reached the landing in tandem, me panting and out of breath, Peter wonderfully invigorated with this new playmate.

"That was fun. What are we going to do now?"

Giving it up as a loss, I stumbled into my room with Peter at my heels. "We're going to find my white blouse so that I can wear it with this skirt I bought." My head was buried in my crimson carry-all bag, handfuls of t-shirts and underwear showering over my shoulder to land on the bed and the floor. "There it is." I pulled out the soiled and wrinkled shirt. "Damnit, it's dirty!"

"Peter?" A young woman stood in the doorway, her gaze wandering over the discarded underclothes scattered haphazardly around Peter.

"Oh hello," I said, blushing under her stare. "Peter has just been, ahh, helping me find something."

A grin broke through her suspicious expression. She reached forward and ruffled Peter's hair. "Peter, have you been bothering the guests again? I'm sorry. My husband is the warden of the hostel, and Peter gets bored when we're busy."

"That's alright. I'm just in a bit of a hurry. I have to be at the cathedral in," I glanced down at my watch, "one hour and I've just discovered this is the only blouse I have to wear." I held up the stained blouse in disgust.

"That looks a bit of a mess, doesn't it?" She reached out and took it. "We can't let you go to church in this, can we, Peter?" Peter jumped up and down and shook his head vigorously back and forth. "I'll do a spot wash and iron it for you."

I closed my eyes and muttered a silent prayer of thanks.

"That would be wonderful, thank you. I'll have just enough time then to have a wash and get dressed."

A quick dash into the shower and then a spell in front of an upturned hand dryer and I was pulling on my clean and pressed clothes. A spritz of some perfume and I was ready to go.

The two of them stood on the hostel doorstep and waved me off down the road. "Have a good time," the young mother shouted after me, "and say a prayer for us."

It had just turned four as I dashed up the narrow lane to the cathedral gate. The scrap of paper Mabel had given me listed an address in an area called the Precinct, which my map gave as a group of church buildings on the cathedral grounds.

I headed around the end of the cathedral and through into a large, grassy quadrangle. A group of red brick buildings in various stages of ruin encircled the common. Two young boys, dressed in Edwardian black tailcoats and stiff white shirts, were playing football on the grass. It took me a few moments to place them as students of the exclusive public school whose buildings are situated within the cathedral grounds and not characters from *Tom Brown's Schooldays*.

"Excuse me, could you tell me where I can find Canon Brett's apartment?"

The older of the two boys pointed in the direction of a small cubbyhole in a crumbling stone wall. "Through there. The first door on the right."

The door was shaped like an anvil and made of a wood so old it had darkened to the colour of deep, dusky pitch. Metal staves with heavy screws joined it to the stone wall. I lifted my hand and knocked, wondering whether a medieval monk might appear in the doorway.

A pleasant looking middle-aged woman opened the door and gestured me into a modern looking interior. "Peter, your four o'clock appointment is here," she called out.

Canon Brett appeared through a doorway to greet me. Tweed-jacketed and balding, he exuded the exact mixture of politeness and warmth you might expect from a vicar. All he needed was a pipe and a Labrador to complete the picture.

He led me into his office and sat me in a chair overlooking the quadrangle.

"So you're a journalist?" he said as he settled himself behind his desk.

I nodded yes and explained that my mission, so to speak, was to travel around Europe writing about the people and places that interested me. This week's column, I added, would look behind the scenes at "Life in the cathedral".

"Fascinating," he murmured and tugged down at the cuffs of his suit jacket before leaning back and meditatively staring at the ceiling. "Life in the cathedral. Well, we have a number of different responsibilities here. We have to try to be a beacon, a beacon of the reality of God to the world, as well as," he gestured to the crumbling buildings around us, "overseeing the history and the architecture of these buildings."

"Do you find your job as a priest overwhelmed by these other responsibilities, being a historian and public relations person in addition to being a vicar?"

"No, not really," he shook his head gently in disagreement. "We do try to be subtle with our message to the people who visit the cathedral. Our job is to try and present that there is something bigger than 'I'; that there is a greater reality."

"Does it bother you that so many people visit the cathedral because of its architecture or its history rather than because it's a house of God?" I asked.

He pondered this, rearranging some pens on his desk. "I remember a young couple who came one day to see the cathedral. They had been married at a registry office, and I don't think they were overly religious. They were so moved by the beauty of the cathedral that they asked a passing priest if he would bless their marriage." He smiled at the memory and shrugged his shoulders at the mystery of faith. "We are content to just try and sow seeds."

The sun was beginning to sink towards the edge of the garden wall. Canon Brett looked down at his desk clock and stood up with a start. "I'm afraid we're going to have to leave now if we're going to make the Evensong service."

The two young boys had disappeared in search of tea, leaving us to wander quietly among the peace of the old buildings. An early evening breeze wafted the scent of roses over the ruins as we passed on the way to the cathedral.

"I'm sorry, but I will have to leave you here," said Canon Brett with regret as we entered a side door. "If you walk down this aisle, you may be able to find a seat beside the choir boys."

I seated myself on a hard wooden pew near the choir and stared up at the intricately vaulted ceiling. The organ began to play with a rousing chord and Canon Brett and the other clergy proceeded down the aisle, each cloaked in richly coloured vestments and wafting incense from a golden holder. As a single pure tenor voice filled the air with song, I closed my eyes and whispered a prayer for a young hostel warden and her mischevious son.

iii wandering with wordsworth ❖❖❖❖

The Lake District. Home to Wordsworth, Coleridge, and those literary fields of daffodils. Four years of English literature studies began to ooze their way out of my pores as I gazed down at the countryside from my seat atop a double decker Cumberland bus.

Richard Wordsworth, a direct descendant of the literary William, was my reason for trekking to the Lake District. This interview, I felt proudly, was quite a coup. A Wordsworthian perspective on the Lake District. My editors would love it. I couldn't help but congratulate myself as the bus rolled out of the station in Windermere and along the road to Grasmere.

We skirted Lake Windermere, where the first tricklings of the summer's tourists bobbed in small boats on the bluish water. What would these roads be like in mid-summer, I wondered, when the Lake District was packed with overflowing Ford Escorts, disgorging rabid twelve-year-olds looking for the loo?

It would be a far sight from the peace and quiet of this sunny May day. And it was sunny, gloriously so, I thought, as I watched the bright yellow light glinting off the peaceful waters.

It was raining by the time we arrived in Grasmere.

"Grasmere," the bus driver shouted as we rolled over a stone bridge and pulled up on the side of a narrow lane. A few hikers stood up and we all migrated to the front of the bus, hesitating as we looked through the open doors at the pelting rain lashing the road outside.

"A hiker, are you?" a male voice asked from behind me as a German couple tentatively stepped out the door.

"Ahh, no," I murmured, my attention focused on the downpour outside.

"Just here to visit then?" the voice persisted.

I turned around. A man in his early twenties stood behind me, his brown hair cropped short and shaggy, his mouth hanging slightly open. With his tall, thin body and pointed features, he looked like an overlarge Irish wolfhound puppy.

"Yes, well, really to work," I replied and took a brave leap out the door. He followed me, blithely ignoring the rain to hover in the street beside me. "I'm trying to find the hostel. Do you know where it is?" I asked as I pulled out my umbrella and popped it open.

He bent half over, folding like a mannequin, to take shelter underneath it. "Yeah, it's just up the road a mile. I'll take you there, if you like."

"Thanks, that would be great."

His smile, if possible, widened. "But first, do you want to pop into the pub for a drink?" He gestured with his thumb to a pub, the Red Lion, across the square.

The bus had disappeared in a shush of water and the other new arrivals had scattered for cover. I felt damp through, and wanted nothing more than a place to dump my bags and take a hot shower. But my new found friend refused to release me from his stare.

"Sure. I'd love a drink," I reluctantly said. He was, after all, going to personally guide me to the hostel. It seemed the decent thing to step out of the rain and share a pint with him.

We dashed through the rain to the entrance of the pub and shook ourselves off in the hall. I seated myself in one corner of the snug, steam rising from my damp clothing. The young man returned with two frothing pints and placed them on the table in front of us.

"By the way, my name is John." A large, long-fingered hand was shoved across the table. I grasped it and found my right hand being shaken so soundly it felt like my arm might be dislocated from my shoulder.

"Kim, Kim Herdman," I replied shakily.

"Nice to meet you, Kim." He glanced around the room with its leather seats and minimal lighting, oozing a palpable air of self satisfaction. When he caught the eye of the elderly barman, he winked.

I took a sip of my lager and stared at a beer mat in disbelief. I glanced up to see he was still examining me with the same pleasure a naturalist displays upon finding a rare beetle species. It would have been revolting if it hadn't been so ludicrously funny. After all, I am no pinup. And yet his pleasure lacked that leering, "I'm going to get laid" quality, and was instead laced with an awkward naivete that was both embarrassing and endearing.

I discovered that John lived in the Lake District and had taken a few days off from his job at a local pulp mill to do some hiking. He was more than a little impressed when told I was a travelling journalist, and seemed to puff up proudly at the thought.

After taking a last pull from my glass, I grabbed my bags and pushed my seat back. My damp clothes still stuck to my body. "It looks like the sun is coming out, John. I'd better be going."

"Sure, I'll take you up to the hostel."

The sun had broken through the leaden cloud cover and the village of Grasmere glistened with a shimmer of rain-wet slate roofs. The post office, noticeable by its bright red and gold sign, funneled rainwater in a steady stream off its awning onto the road.

At the edge of town, I spotted a youth hostel sign pointing up the road and dropped my bags on the damp earth.

"Well, thanks for all your help, John." I thrust my hand out in farewell.

A horrified look spread across his face. "But this isn't the hostel. We've still got a ways to go," he sputtered out.

"I know, but the sign says it's just a half mile up this road. I can make it by myself."

With a dismissive shake of his head, John stepped past me and hoisted my bags onto his shoulder. "That's okay. I don't mind walking you the whole way." With a broad grin on his face, he started up the road without me.

I couldn't believe it. Nothing but a runaway bus was going to get rid of this man. I picked up my remaining bag and ran up the road after him, ducking under the overhanging tree branches that dripped down onto the road.

The hostel lay in a small valley, surrounded on all sides by a well-tended spring garden. The old house with its bay windows looked all the more welcoming because I knew it contained the one amenity I desperately needed: a hot shower.

John was several feet in front of me as we reached the front door. With a thump from one bony hip, he threw the doors open and clomped in his heavy hiking boots to the front desk.

"Hi. Do you have any beds for tonight?" he asked with a maddening air of authority.

I shouldered my way up to the desk and fixed John with what I hoped was a pleasant but firm stare. "Thanks, John. I can handle it from here. I'd like a bed for three nights, please."

The white-haired warden had watched this exchange with a quizzical smile. "A bed for one? Or two?"

"One," I stated firmly.

"I see." He ran his finger down the list. "Hmm, we're pretty full right now, but I can fit you in for the next two nights."

"What about Friday night?"

The warden shook his head no. "It's the beginning of the bank holiday weekend. Everything is full."

I handed him my youth hostel card and signed in for the two nights regardless, pulling my wet shirt away from where it stuck to the middle of my back. "Is it possible for me to have a shower? I'm wet through."

"Sorry, the hostel is closed. The most I can do is let you take your bags up to your room and dry off. After that I'm afraid you'll have to leave until the hostel opens in," he swiveled his watch, "three and a half hours."

John leapt on this statement like a hound after a meaty bone. "You can come up with me to Easedale Tarn. I was planning on hiking there today anyway."

"Easedale Tarn is a beautiful hike," added the warden, nodding his approval. "And the weather's certainly improved this afternoon."

"Lovely," I muttered through gritted teeth as I headed for the staircase.

After a brisk rub down and a change into dry clothes, I headed off with John to Easedale Tarn. The scenery was certainly breathtaking. Rich green hills rolled in waves of spongy green grass down to narrow streams edged with wildflowers. Sheep dotted the landscape like furry signposts. It almost made up for having to listen to John's continuous droning monologue.

Almost.

His life appeared to revolve around his job at the pulp mill and his after hours hobby of studying the American Civil War. I am not, and never have been, a Civil War buff. Quite frankly, I have a tendency to confuse Gettysburg with the Battle of Waterloo and have been known to happily toast Napoleon's defeat when the former is mentioned. It appeared that John was used to people who knew even less about the Civil War than I did and so with the occasional, "And I suppose Lee was involved there?", I managed to look like a dyed-in-the-wool historian.

We trekked along a well-worn earthen path that led to a distant waterfall, a particular favourite of Dorothy and William Wordsworth. Sheep calmly examined us as we climbed over the stone fences. The only trouble we encountered was when I tried to photograph an old ram. When he began to snort and paw the ground, I retreated in a hurry to find that John had failed to even notice my disappearance. From a distance, I could still hear him murmuring on about battlefield casualties in Pennsylvania in 1863.

Pleading exhaustion, I finally deposited John in the village and returned alone to the hostel. I foolishly thought that I would never see him again.

The next morning dawned with a glorious sunrise, all signs of inclement weather gone. Forecasts on the romantic front were also propitious. John was nowhere to be seen. I headed off alone to speak to Dr. Robert Woof, the Director of the Wordsworth Trust.

I found Dr. Woof waiting for me in the foyer of the Wordsworth Museum, a young Oxford acolyte hovering beside him in a three piece suit. A world renowned scholar, Dr. Woof was also a much sought-after lecturer in addition to his duties as director of the trust. Short and bespectacled with a messy cap of brown hair, he was hardly heart-throb material; but his grasp was warm and firm and there was definitely something attractive about his rumpled tweed jacket and soft academic voice.

"Hello, Kim. It's lovely to meet you. This is my assistant, Nigel. I'm afraid I have some pressing appointments today, so we don't have a great deal of time."

I nodded my head like a goggle eyed teenager with a crush on her new poetry teacher. He was a bit old perhaps, but what a mind!

As we headed off into the museum, Robert, as he had asked to be called, delved into the intricacies of the Romantic period. I scribbled down details and added the occasional literary comment, trying to remember points from long past poetry lectures.

He probably has a wife, I reasoned. But then he may be divorced. That would be a positive sign. Single at his age was too much to ask for. Unless he was gay. I pushed that thought to the back of my mind.

"And this is our Wordsworth section." Robert stopped in front of a display case which held several handwritten manuscripts. "You can see a particularly illuminating passage of his work here." He pointed to a poem penned in fading ink and began to recite a portion from memory.

A young couple came to a stop beside us, unsure whether this was an organized tour or an impromptu declaration of love from an aging suitor. I didn't care what they thought. I was throroughly enjoying my recitation.

Suddenly, Nigel appeared beside us. "Robert." He tapped on his shoulder with polite insistence. "You've got a lunch appointment, remember?"

Robert paused, like an actor in mid-breath, and looked at Nigel with a mixture of irritation and sheepishness. "I can still make it. Don't worry, Nigel. We'll just have to move a bit faster." Grabbing my arm, he moved us on to the next exhibit.

But if anything, we began to move more slowly. We had arrived at Robert's specialty, the poetry of William Wordsworth. Letters, books, everything that pertained to Wordsworth's work was displayed. But despite my respect for Robert's knowledge, I had to admit that he was rambling on a bit. Like a true academic, he was incapable of using a single sentence when he could use three. We had progressed not more than a few feet before Nigel reappeared, cellular phone at the ready, desperation etched across his face.

"Robert? Your lunch date?" he repeated with a pained expression.

With a sigh, Robert turned to face him. "Just cancel it, Nigel."

"Cancel?" This was obviously a new word in Nigel's vocabulary.

"Yes, cancel. I'll have lunch here and then move on to my afternoon appointment." Robert turned me towards the next display.

"But, but, Robert, you know you can't miss this afternoon's appointment." Nigel trailed anxiously behind us. "It's very important."

"I know, Nigel. I won't."

We continued our leisurely examination of the museum and then wandered out into the noonday sun. I scanned the garden for a glimpse of Nigel popping up behind the rose bushes with his cellular phone in one hand and a glass of Alka Seltzer in the other, but saw nothing.

"Would you like to join me for lunch?" Robert asked.

"Yes, I'd love to."

We were halfway through our soup when Nigel appeared at the entrance to the restaurant and, after a furtive glance around the room, made eye contact with us. He pointed at his watch and then outside at the car. We watched this unique semaphore for a few moments before Robert laid down his spoon and stood up.

"I'm afraid I really will have to go," he said with, I felt, a note of regret. "Please stay if you'd like. I will cover the bill."

With a quick squeeze of my hand, he disappeared out the door with Nigel trotting happily behind him. I was left with an empty seat and a half-eaten bowl of vegetable soup.

The next morning, with bags in hand, I left the hostel en route for Derwentwater, a small town further north which still had beds available in its hostel. To my surprise and irritation, John was waiting at the bus stop.

"Good morning, Kim," he said chirpily.

"What are you doing here?"

"Waiting for you. Do you want to go and get some breakfast?"

Frustration flooded up inside my body and then slowly ebbed away. He was exactly like a Wolfhound puppy, oblivious to any and all destruction, intent only on chasing balls and being happy.

"No, I've eaten. I'm here to catch the bus."

John nodded his head knowingly. "I thought you would be. You know, since you couldn't stay in Grasmere another night. Where are you going?"

This time I was not going to be caught out.

"Where are you going?" I asked warily.

John hesitated and then added with a smile, "Wherever you're going."

The bus bound for Keswick and my connection on to Derwentwater ground its way out of second gear and chugged up the main street.

"Here comes the bus for Keswick. Is that the one you want?" John asked.

I had no choice. "Yes."

"Good. I haven't been up to Keswick in a long time." He picked up all of our bags and stepped up into the double decker bus, leaving me to follow dispiritedly in his wake.

A larger and more commercial town than Grasmere, Keswick rests on the north shore of Derwentwater, one of the largest lakes in England. We disembarked from our bus at the bus loop in the center of town and John disappeared in search of a bathroom. I asked the driver when the next bus to Derwentwater would be leaving.

He glanced up at the sky as if he could read the timetable there. "Bout an hour, I'd say. Why don't you walk? It's not that long a trip."

I had been hoping to make a quick escape. "Thanks. I think I'll wait for the bus."

Five minutes later, John reappeared with two garishly coloured, sticky ice cream cones. He thrust one into my hand and took a long lick at his own.

"Thanks, John, but I don't want an ice cream cone." I pushed it back with more force than was necessary. He looked hurt, and I felt a pang of guilt.

"I bought it for you. I don't want two, and anyway it's dripping." He pushed it back at me and I, hating myself for giving in, took the gloppy confection. Normally I like ice cream, but this mixture was sickly sweet and disgusting.

"John, I think we'd better say goodbye now."

"Why? I can show you where the hostel is here."

"No, I don't need the hostel here," I said, hoping my vagueness would discourage further questions.

"Why?"

"Because I'm not staying in Keswick."

He took another sloppy lick at his pink ice cream. "Where are you staying?"

It was no use. "Derwentwater."

"Oh," he brightened at this, "the hostel at Derwentwater. I can take you there."

"Thank you, John, but I don't want you to take me there. I'm waiting for the bus, and I can make it on my own."

"But it's only a short walk."

"I'd prefer to take the bus."

"Oh don't be ridiculous. The bus won't be coming for a long time. We can walk there before the bus even arrives."

I made a grab for my bags, knowing what to expect, but John managed to get hold of one of them first. He was headed off down the main street before I could call out after him.

"John, stop! I'm going to take the bus! Give me back my bag!"

He ignored me, and a cluster of women with shopping bags slung over their wrists turned to stare. Lovers tiff, they probably thought, or perhaps one of those deranged people from the city having a fit.

With a fresh wave of anger crashing over me, I ran after John. With my other bags in tow, it took me a while to catch up with him. This time I didn't even try to conceal my anger.

"John, I told you I was going to take the bus. Why didn't you stop?"

He laughed. "Because that's silly. It's such a short walk. We'll be there in no time. You'll see." He turned off the road and cut across a field.

"But John, that's not the point!" I called out, but he wasn't listening. I could hear him mumbling on about the issue of cotton prices in regards to the South's military position.

The short walk turned out to be a two mile hike, most of it over rough fields and along a stretch of deserted beach. I was hot, tired, and dirty by the time we reached the main road again. And I was very, very angry.

"Have you ever thought of studying history at university, John?" I asked.

"University? I'm not bright enough for that."

"Well, you certainly sound like you know quite a bit," I said. He blushed a brilliant crimson. "You know, you can go to university at any age. My fiancé is going to university right now, and he must be older than you are."

John halted dead in his tracks and stopped talking. For the first time, I could hear the beautiful silence of the Lake District. "Fiancé?"

"Yes, didn't I mention him before?"

"No." John's conversational skills had dried up. I was angry enough not to care. The fact that I didn't have a fiancé, or even a boyfriend, didn't stir my conscience.

"Yes, he's brilliant. A real scholar. He's working towards his masters in philosophy. Probably become a professor."

"A professor," John repeated dully.

"Oh yes, and I miss him so much," I continued on, callously driving further nails into poor John's heart. "He's in France right now, and I'll be meeting up with him soon." I gave an over-dramatic sigh and glanced at John. His footsteps had slowed and his constant smile tipped towards a grimace. A twinge of guilt worked its way through my stomach.

"That's nice. Oh, this is the hostel here," he murmured.

We stopped at a drive winding up to a cream-coloured building. John dropped my bags onto the ground. "It was nice meeting you, Kim," he murmured.

I couldn't believe it. I felt terrible. I had to fight the desire to invite him up to the hostel for a restorative cup of tea. "And it was nice meeting you, John."

He looked in my eyes for a second and then, with a sudden movement, kissed me firmly on the lips with a loud smack. He turned on his heel and headed quickly up the road into town, leaving me standing on the asphalt feeling like I had heartlessly run over a defenseless puppy.

The small Volvo drove up the gravel drive of the lodge and ground to a halt. A frail, thin man emerged hesitantly from the side seat. Richard Wordsworth had sounded quite intimidating over the telephone, insisting on not more than a half-hour interview. In person, he appeared quite the opposite, fragile and older than I had expected. His wavy hair and long, thick beard were pure white, as was his suit. Only his crimson cravat added a splash of colour to his face.

"I suppose you're the journalist?" he asked as he made his way towards me with the aid of a cane.

"Yes, I am, Mr. Wordsworth."

He waved his hand in the air, as if brushing my words away. "Richard, dear, it's Richard. Here, we'll go up to the lodge to talk."

His manner, far from being intimidating, was foppish and theatrical. We seated ourselves in the sitting room of the hotel, which belonged to the Wordsworth Trust and was decorated in a plush Victorian style. I laid out my notebook and pens on the red velvet sofa beside me.

"Oh dear, I suppose you need all those things, don't you?" Richard said with a grimace, and nodded to a young man who was hovering in the doorway. "Peter, we'd like some tea, please. Tea all right with you, dear?"

I said that it would be fine.

"You're sure you wouldn't prefer coffee?"

"No, really, tea is fine."

With a nod, Richard settled himself back in a wingback chair, his cane propped up in front of him.

"First off, Mr. Wordsworth, sorry, Richard, could you tell me a little bit about your life, your career?"

Richard smiled broadly and relaxed in his chair. "My career," he chuckled. "Now that's a bit of a story."

It turned out that his theatrical air had been come by honestly - he had once made his living as an actor. After moving to London as a young man, he had worked at the Old Vic with John Gielgud and travelled with their productions around the world. In later years, his one man show, *The Bliss of Solitude*, had played in many different countries.

"They luvvv me in the United States, honey," he said in a thick southern drawl and then paused, with an actor's timing, for my laughter.

"What brought you back to the Lake District?"

"When I retired, I decided to move back here. I grew up here, in Grasmere and at Rydal Mount, the Wordsworth house a few miles away from here. It's always been my home."

"So what do you do with your time now?"

With a flamboyant turn, Richard twirled the cane in his hands so that its bottom spun on the carpet. "I interest myself in matters Wordsworthian," he said and nodded to his teacup.

Playing mother, I poured out a stream of amber tea and handed the cup to him.

His Wordsworthian duties included helping the Wordsworth Trust, the organization that preserves Wordsworth buildings and memorabilia. As part of his job, he had started a popular summer literature conference that brings together scholars on the Romantic period along with interested participants for two weeks of seminars.

"It's not just lectures though, pet." The atmosphere between us had warmed to the extent that he now called me "pet". "We also take walks and do tours of the countryside. Seamus Heaney will be here again this year."

"Seamus Heaney? He's one of my favourite poets."

"What a shame you can't be here. We do have some fun in the pub with old Seamus." Richard cast an appraising eye over my physique and then grinned. "And he does have a love for wine, women and song, does our Seamus."

With a blush, I turned to the next question. "What was it like growing up with William Wordsworth as an ancestor?"

Richard thought about this for a moment. "When I was a child, I would much rather he'd been a famous footballer. I remember one day at school, I suddenly realized that the original copy of the book we were studying was sitting on the shelf in my family's house. I realized then that I had to share my family, my past, with the world."

With a glance at my notebook, I realized that I had exhausted my list of questions and had filled several pages with notes. "Thank you for your time, Richard. I've kept you here much longer than I said I would."

"Really? It's over?" His face fell. "I was enjoying our little chat."

I moved to stand up and he shakily joined me. "Are you staying in town?"

"No, I'm staying in Derwentwater. I'm just going to go and have some lunch in town and then head back there," I said as we made our way down the stone path that connected the lodge to Dove Cottage.

"May I walk with you into town? I'm supposed to be meeting my wife there," he asked shyly.

I agreed and we headed off along the road into the village, chatting about our favourite authors. When we came level with the church, Richard hesitated. "Have you seen Dorothy and William's graves yet?"

I said no, and he gestured me into the church. "You really must see them before you go."

The graves were easy to spot. Three woman were clustered around them, pointing at the stones and chatting among themselves. We stepped past the group and Richard halted in front of two other stones.

"These are my mother and father."

In my left ear, I could hear the group of women talking about Wordsworth and poetry and "Ooh, isn't it lovely here, but food is a bit dear." I looked up at Richard's aging face. It had lost its theatrical joviality. We waited in silence until the group left.

"Does it bother you that you have to share something private like this with the world?"

He shrugged his shoulders, as if to say he was used to it.

I surreptitiously examined Richard's face as we quietly hovered in front of the gravestones. I had met three very different men during my stay in Grasmere and had wasted so much time on affairs of the heart that I'd almost forgotten what had brought me here. Perhaps it was only fitting then that my visit should conclude in this churchyard with Richard. As his famous ancestor, a world class poet, once wrote:

Strange fits of passion have I known;
And I will dare to tell,
But in the Lover's ear alone,
What once to me befell.

iv scotland: sex, drugs and sheep

I spent my first three days in Scotland closeted on the top floor of a teetering Edinburgh bed and breakfast. Since I had visited there on a previous trip, I already knew the castle and the palace, the tartan shops of Princes Street and the green cliffs of the city. Now, all I wanted was to be left alone to write my first batch of columns. I had not counted on the constant interruptions of the landlady's alcoholic lover.

Oozing Scottish charm, he served me wonderful breakfasts: bowls full of oatmeal, oval dinner plates piled high with sausages, eggs and thin strips of ham, a symmetrical row of toast cooling in the rack. His cooking was marvellous, as was the peace of having a breakfast room, indeed the entire house, to myself.

The landlady never appeared in the morning, which was a shame as it was probably her only chance to see her boyfriend sober. Forgetful, perhaps, looking a bit worn and tired, definitely, but always sober. By the time she surfaced in mid-afternoon, his thick accent had turned guttural and his cheeks had brightened to an unnaturally rosy shade.

At about nine in the evening, after several hours in the pub, he would come home and shout three floors up the staircase: "Missy Herdman. Missy Herdman!"

Peering over the bannister, I could see him swaying, one hand clinging to the shiny post, on the bottom floor. "Did you have a nice day today, Missy Herdman?"

I locked my door carefully each night.

With the first batch of columns finished, I bid Edinburgh good bye and chugged off on the train for Glasgow, en route to the Isle of Lewis and Harris. After a warm welcome from the Glasgow Tourist Board, I checked in to the hostel and headed up to relax in my room. Two young women were thumbing through a photo album on the bunk beside mine. Their names were Nat and Van.

Van, tall with a dark, Mediterranean attractiveness, spoke first in a thick Australian twang. "Hi. Are you staying in this room?"

When I said yes, Nat reached into her bottom bunk and proffered a package of biscuits. She, too, spoke with an Australian accent. "Would you like a bickie?"

I took one out of the package and climbed up on my bunk.

Nat was shorter than Van, pretty in an English way, with shoulder-length blondish curls and aqua-colored eyes. She looked you straight in the eye when she spoke, with a directness that suggested a strong personality. Van seemed more shy, but friendly, with a warm, bubbly laugh.

"How long are you in Glasgow for?" Van asked as I, taking part in the sharing ritual that is part of hostel life, passed around a roll of candies.

"Just till tomorrow. I'm staying over to see the city before continuing on up north."

"Us too. We just stopped here so we could see a girl we met when we were travelling through Thailand." Nat pointed to a photo of a sweating girl standing in what looked like a Thai jungle. "Here she is. Agnes. We're having dinner with her tonight, and then going out for a drink."

It turned out that Nat and Van, like so many peripatetic Aussies and Kiwis, were travelling around the world. Forced by southern isolation, they had joined that annual migration of young people from Down Under. True to form, Nat and Van were travelling the Australian way, sightseeing until their money ran out, then getting temporary jobs until they could afford to continue. They were now headed for Ireland, where they hoped to find a few months work.

Van swung her long, tanned legs around so that they dangled over her bunk and swayed in front of Nat's face. A friendly slap from Nat and she drew them up again. "I've got an idea. Why don't you come out with us tonight?"

I hesitated at interfering with their reunion.

"Come on, why don't you?" Nat chipped in. "Agnes won't mind. We'll have dinner with her and then come back and pick you up."

Their Australian enthusiasm was infectious. I said yes.

Agnes was sitting on Van's bunk when I returned to the room after dinner. She looked very different from the sarong-clad girl in the photo. Dressed all in black, from a lace dress to heavy stockings and work boots, she looked like a punk rocker on her way to a funeral. But her face, with its blonde hair and bright smile, contradicted this macabre image.

We caught a bus into the centre of the city and made our way to a pub called the Corn Exchange. It looked more like a wine bar than a pub, with its yuppie gold and glass interior, but the miasma of smoke was the same, as was the crush of people.

We were immediately hailed by a group of young people at a table. Hugs and kisses were exchanged, and I was introduced to all as "Kim, a friend of Nat and Van". The four of us squeezed into some extra seats around the table, and a young man was dispatched to the bar for a round of drinks. I felt ancient and boring, seated among these young people. Despite the working class character of

Glasgow, they were all fashionably dressed with a European trendiness. Not for them the world of running shoes and backpacks. They all wore leather shoes and most of the men wore fashionably cut blazers.

Only one of them had a job.

"Are you at school?" I asked the young man sitting beside me. It turned out he was eighteen and had never been to college or had a job.

"I've never been to college either," his friend added. "Hope to get on a training scheme though. Both of us do."

It was a common story. What was the use of higher education? It doesn't help you fill out the form for the dole, does it? Agnes was working, but in a job she hated. She was a rarity and, I noticed, the only one with a full wallet. Despite their problems, the group kindly wouldn't allow me to buy my own drinks. I was glad when we left the bar for the more democratic territory of a new nightclub.

Buried in the depths of a downtown warehouse, the club shook to a rhythmic acid house beat. The clean, primary colours of the dance floor were swamped in darkness, the only light coming from the throbbing strobes that turned the dancers into surreal, almost grotesque, figures. In the bathroom, young women, giggling, queued up to file into the stalls. They reappeared a few moments later. A caretaker sat in a corner of the washroom in a worn cotton dress. She watched us with a smile as we fiddled with our hair, and then shot a sad glance at a young girl listing her way to the door.

Our party, which had now swelled to over twenty, was seated at a table far from the dance floor. As we walked over to join them, I could see Agnes accepting a plastic package from a young man. She saw us approaching and pulled him to her for a kiss, surreptitiously dropping whatever he had given her into her lap.

"Why isn't anybody dancing?" asked Nat.

Glazed eyes stared up at us.

"Don't really feel like it, Nat," Agnes answered softly.

Nat, Van and I took to the dance floor, swirling around in the bizarre half light, bodies moving to the driving beat. The club's acid house music was worse than the disco I remembered from my teenage "Staying Alive" days. It consisted of nothing but ten-minute-long symphonies by drum machines. A Concerto in Electronics. Everyone danced alone, each person on the floor cocooned in his or her own private world. A girl with green hair stood rooted to the middle of the dance floor, eyes closed, occasionally waving her hands in front of her face.

I was out of my depth.

There was a quick hug and kiss from Agnes as we piled into the taxi to take us back to the hostel. The girls shouted out plans for lunch the next day as the cab pulled away from the curb.

"We were the only people in that club who weren't on drugs, you know," Nat offered as we drove along the rain-slick streets.

"I know," I agreed. "But what I can't understand is why Agnes tried to hide it from us."

"I didn't even know Agnes did drugs," Van said. "She didn't when we were in Thailand together. I mean, we all got pissed occasionally, but that was it."

"It's different here," Nat said sadly. "She's different here. Agnes told me that she didn't want us to know. She said we didn't need to know it, we didn't need it, you know, the drugs."

"Why?" Van asked.

Nat nodded to the sooty, decaying buildings on either side of the road. "Because we don't have to live here."

* * *

Through the fogged windows of the boat, I could see the Isle of Skye bobbing murkily in the distance. I gripped a warm mug of tea in my hands in a vain attempt to regain circulation in my fingertips while the rain banged with wind-driven force on the roof of the ferry. I had not expected summer weather, but this was ridiculous.

Once on Skye, even my valiant umbrella could not protect me from the rain. I was soaked to the skin by the time the bus to the hostel arrived. An hour later, we were disgorged in the tiny town of Kyleakin and I staggered, blue-lipped, to the hostel.

After dumping my bags, I hurried to the hostel kitchen to cook myself something warm for dinner. As I emptied a casserole mix into a pot, I looked up to find a man standing beside me, cooking something on the other burner.

"Hello," I said.

He looked up and smiled. He was older than most of the other hostellers, with short brown hair and a moustache flecked with a few hairs of grey. His eyes were hazel and friendly and his cream roll-neck sweater gave him a faintly nautical look.

"Hello," he answered in a soft accent.

"What part of the States are you from?" I prided myself on my ability to distinguish accents.

He laughed and popped a tinfoil tray into the oven. "I'm not from the States. I'm from Canada."

I hooted in embarrassment. "Sorry about that. I'm from Canada, too. Everyone mistakes me for an American, and here I am doing the same thing. My name's Kim. Kim Herdman."

"Tom Kraft."

It turned out that, although I grew up in Vancouver, we both had family living in the same small town in Eastern Canada.

"You can't have family that live there. Nobody lives there!"

"Well, my uncle did," Tom said.

"I don't believe it!" I mentioned a family name and saw him nod his head in recognition. "I can't believe I've just met someone, in a hostel on the Isle of Skye, that I'm related to!"

"Not by blood," Tom cautioned as we picked up our dinners and retreated to the dining area to eat.

It didn't strike either of us, at the time, how significant that distinction might one day become.

A thirty-five-year-old unemployed engineer, Tom was beginning a long-awaited tour of Europe. We compared travelling notes and laughed over our shared misfortunes of missed trains and bad weather. Somehow the rain thrumming outside the hostel no longer seemed to be the malevolent power it had been a few hours earlier.

Satisfied and warm, I scraped up the last mouthful of my dinner and picked up my empty plate. "It was nice talking to you, Tom. Maybe I'll see you later?"

I thought I detected a flash of regret on his face. "Oh, sure. I'm heading back to Glasgow tomorrow morning and then on to Ireland next week. But, you never know, we might meet up again sometime."

What a shame I'll probably never see him again, I thought as I climbed up the stairs to my room. Not my type, of course, but a nice person to talk to on a rainy night.

Lots of tourists get killed around here." The ticket collector said as he stopped in the aisle of the bus and gripped a headrest. He nodded at the narrow winding road. "Specially at this time of year."

I looked out the window and wondered if I would ever make it to the Isle of Lewis and Harris. The early morning bus to Uig, the departure point from Skye for Lewis and Harris, dipped and swooped along the narrow roads. I could understand why people preferred to leave the driving to someone else. This thought was seconded by the ticket collector when he wandered back to check on my destination.

"Happens every year, you know. Foreigners, that's who it is. Come here, drive too fast, and then flip." He made a rolling gesture with his hand and smacked the top of his fist onto the armrest. "That's the end of them."

I thought his fascination for auto accidents was rather morbid, especially considering his line of work. "What about bus accidents?" I asked.

He shrugged his shoulders impassively. "It happens, but not that often. And when it does, you can be sure it's not our fault."

Somehow that didn't reassure me.

The ferry trip from Uig to Lewis and Harris lasted three hours, long enough for me to enjoy a snooze in the cabin. What had initially confused me about this island in the Outer Hebrides was the communal blindness its inhabitants have towards the fact that both Harris and Lewis are actually a single land mass. Joined through the middle by a mountain range, the citizens of Lewis and Harris still feel they occupy separate worlds, as distant as though the choppy Irish Sea bisects them. Perhaps it has something to do with the fact that a large part of Harris has been in private ownership since the thirteenth century. Or perhaps it is just good old Celtic stubborness.

Tarbert, the ferry port on North Harris reminded me of a Newfoundland fishing village, with small wooden buildings in a variety of colours tumbling down to the tiny dock area. The rest of the bay is nothing more than a water-filled slit between granite boulders. As the hardy handful of visitors trooped off the ferry, an inquisitive sheep watched from the main street. When we had finished disembarking, she turned with an air of boredom and trotted back into town.

"Mary, we've got a journalist here!"

The tourist office was situated in a tiny, ramshackle bungalow a few feet from the dock. The two middle-aged women put aside their knitting as I entered the single room.

"Yes, yes, she wants a place to stay," said the pudgy woman behind the desk. Her cheeks were red-veined, most likely from the constant wind that whips over the island. "How about Mrs. MacLeod? Do you think that's a good idea, Mary?"

Mary agreed.

"Would you like to stay at Mrs. MacLeod's house?" It didn't strike her that I might not know Mrs. MacLeod. I nodded my head yes.

"Oh good, she's a nice widow. Lives not far from here. And you're here to ...?" The question was left casually unfinished.

"I'm interviewing Anne Campbell of Clo Mor."

"Oh, yes, Clo Mor. So you're here about the tweed."

"That's right," I nodded, "I'm here about the tweed."

The elderly Mrs. MacLeod lived in a small but cosy cottage on the western side of the island. Her accent, like that of the women in the tourist office, was clotted with harsh ullulal sounds that were more Swedish than Scots. Like most of the people on the island, she still spoke Gaelic as her primary tongue. Her English was understandable but shaky.

She showed me to a large upstairs bedroom and then retreated back into her kitchen from where I could hear an English soap opera on the television. I wondered how she picked up the signal. Perhaps some modern innovations had managed to reach Harris. From the murky colour of the bath water, I guessed that proper plumbing was not one of them.

The following day I needed a taxi to take me to my interview with Anne Campbell. There was no taxi service on the island but, so I had been told, Paul, the garage owner, would drive people around. Mrs. MacLeod telephoned for me, the entire conversation a guttural conglomeration of consonants. She hung up the phone and told me he would arrive in a few minutes.

Half an hour later, an old red Fiat pulled to a stuttering stop in front of the house. Mrs. MacLeod opened the door and shouted a greeting in Gaelic. It sounded like an Olde English epithet.

Paul pried himself out of the car and walked up to the front door. "Good morning," he said awkwardly to me and then turned in relief to Mrs. MacLeod, whom he spoke to in a flood of Gaelic.

"I've told him where you want to go," she informed me as I climbed in beside Paul. "Have a nice day."

We headed away from town, the road a single tarmac lane. This soon turned to gravel, and the landscape around us became more and more lunar. Granite mounds rolled and heaved out of the earth, patched with a sparse, scrubby grass. And everywhere there were sheep. Sheep on the road, sheep on the hills, sheep everywhere but behind the wheel of a car. They were obviously the dominant force in the economy of this island.

Conversation with Paul was hesitant.

"Where are you from?" he asked.

"Canada, " I said and explained what I was doing on Harris.

"Yes, Mrs. MacLeod told me. You want to go and see Anne Campbell."

"That's right. At Clo Mor. The Harris tweed weaver."

Paul latched on to the end of my sentence and nodded his head. "Yes, the Harris tweed weaver."

We slipped back into silence. I looked down at my watch. We had been looping and weaving along this narrow track for almost 20 minutes, and yet Clo Mor was only three miles from town. My worries deepened when Paul began to mumble to himself in Gaelic.

"Here," he burst out in English as we bumped and jolted up an all but invisible drive. "Here is Anne Campbell." He looked at me and smiled. "The Harris tweed weaver."

A broad-chested older man was wandering around in front of the old cottage, the stripes on his worn sweater stretching to encompass his size. He walked up to the car and spoke in Gaelic to Peter. He seemed surprised at our arrival.

After a brief consultation, both men turned to look at me with worried expressions on their faces. "This is the husband of Anne Campbell. She is not waiting to see you," said Paul in rebuke.

I pushed past Paul and spoke directly to the man who was now leaning against the car, enjoying this unexpected drama. "I have an appointment with Anne Campbell of Clo Mor for this morning. I spoke to her on the phone yesterday to make sure. She is expecting me."

The man put back his head and hooted in laughter. A rush of Gaelic poured out of his mouth. Paul looked confused. "You want the young Anne Campbell, the one who lives at Clo Mor?" the man repeated to me.

"Yes," I agreed emphatically.

"No," said Paul. "This is the Anne Campbell here, the Harris tweed weaver."

"No, Paul," the man said in English. "She wants the young Anne who lives on the other side of the island. The one who was not born here. She's a weaver too. She was trained by my wife. My wife," he explained to me, "has retired now. Anne has taken over. It's the young Anne Campbell, Peter."

"But she's not the Campbell from Harris," Paul insisted with dogged stubborness.

"I know, but she's the one you want."

With a grumble, we reversed onto the road and set off back towards town. Paul continued to grumble in Gaelic, occasionally turning to me to say, "She's not the Campbell from Harris."

Forty minutes late for my interview, we finally arrived at Clo Mor. It consisted of a small crofter's cottage nestled down near the water with a smaller shed closer to the road. A young woman dressed in ratty jeans and wellington boots stood shyly beside the shed.

"Thanks, Paul," I said as I climbed out. "You can come back for me in an hour or so."

"I won't go," Paul said simply.

I stopped, seeing pound notes slipping from between my fingers. "It's alright, Paul. You don't have to stay."

"I'll stay," he said. "I'll wait at the end of the drive for you."

And with that he pulled my door shut and rocketed up the rutted drive. I turned and approached the young woman. She was tall with a bright, snub-nosed face and mannishly short hair that had not seen a proper cut in a long time. Her voice was soft, with only a trace of the Gaelic accent.

"I'm sorry I'm so late," I apologized as she led me into the shed, "but I'm afraid my driver got you confused with the other Anne Campbell."

"Oh, I see. Old Anne Campbell from Harris?" she asked, immediately understanding the mix-up.

"Yes. They kept on repeating that you're not from here."

Anne laughed. "That's right. I was born on Lewis, the other part of this island. That makes me a bit of a foreigner."

The shed was cold and damp and had a pungent, wild odour. A large loom stood in the middle of it. An assortment of earthy coloured bolts of tweed, in flecked blues and brown tones, were stacked around it on some old tables.

"This is the loom here. It's one of the last in all of the islands, at least here on Harris," Anne said, and sat down behind it.

As she spoke, she began to weave with a pull of her arm and a thump of her foot, the lengths of wool trapped between the cotton threads. Although born in these islands, she had left, like so many others, to attend school in Edinburgh. After working in the city for several years, she had packed in her job and returned home to learn the traditional craft of Harris tweed weaving.

Although Harris tweed is still being woven throughout the islands, the traditional way - using natural wool and herbal dyes, weaving by hand and treating the finished product in the centuries old manner - has all but disappeared. Anne had been taught by one of the only remaining traditional weavers.

"I think if I hadn't come back, Harris tweed actually woven here on Harris would have been finished. It's not something you can read from books and then do. You have to be taught it, you have to learn how to find the moss and then make the dye colors. It's an art," said Anne.

It also looked like a hard life. The crofter's cottage was sparsely decorated and bitterly cold, as was the shed. It was a life that lacked most of the polish and comfort that I take for granted. And yet she seemed happy.

"We pick our own lichens, dye the wool, do everything." I saw a shadowy male figure flit past the cottage and understood the quickly spoken "we". "We do everything in its season. We sell all the tweed we make, which isn't a lot, to places all over the world."

I left her at the loom, working away on a half-finished bolt of fabric. Paul, true to his word, was waiting at the end of the drive. I climbed in and he shoved a protesting gearshift into first. We bounced back up the road.

"It was she you wanted?" he asked suspiciously after a few moments of silence.

"Yes, it was," I replied, rubbing the the soft portion of Harris tweed I had bought between my thumb and forefinger.

Paul shook his head. "She's not the Anne Campbell from Harris."

I nodded my head with a sigh. "I know, Paul. But she's the Harris tweed weaver *I* want."

"Harris tweed weaver," Paul repeated. "Humph."

We finished the journey into town in companionable silence.

v hitching on skye ❖❖❖❖❖❖❖❖❖

I stood at the stern of the ferry and watched as the granite island of Lewis and Harris disappeared on the horizon. It had taken me three days of constant travel, of bitter rain and cold winds to reach this island, only to have the sun return with quixotic pleasure as I departed on the boat.

There was a shuffle of footsteps behind me and I turned to find a middle-aged man standing there, his pea-coloured jacket flapping open in the wind.

"Mark, what are you doing here?"

I had met Mark over sausages and eggs that morning at our bed and breakfast, Mrs. MacLeod's cottage. Mark worked for the Ministry of Defense and had been checking a radio transmitter on Harris.

"What do you think? Going the same place you are, back to the mainland." He laughed and pulled his coat tighter around his body. His face looked like that of an Irish boxer, square with small blue eyes and a squat nose, his strawberry blonde hair blowing erratically in the wind. "You were able to get your interview done in time then? I thought you were going to catch the late ferry."

I told him about my escapade with Paul, the garage owner.

"How are you getting across Skye?" he asked in his thick northern English accent.

I grimaced. "Catching buses, like usual."

"Would you like a lift?"

I hesitated. Hitching was dangerous, but a ride would save so much time over the bus. "Thanks, that would be wonderful."

"Great, I'm just going to get some lunch. I'll see you down on the deck when we're ready to land? Mine is the white Cortina, near the back."

I thanked him again and found a sunny seat on the deck to rest and enjoy the freshness of the breeze. When the landing announcement crackled over the speakers, I trekked down to the car deck. Having been too embarrassed to explain that I had no idea what his British made Cortina actually looked like, I stood awkwardly examining all the white cars. A pea coloured jacket sleeve emerged from a car window and waved at me.

"Couldn't find me, huh?" Mark laughed as he pushed open the passenger door and I clambered in.

"Yeah, sorry."

I did up the seat belt as the ferry pulled in with a loud clunk and rolling swell to the dock at Uig. We slowly motored off, and I looked with malicious pleasure at the handful of young people standing at the edge of the dock waiting for the bus into town. No buses for me today.

Mark fiddled with the radio and then gave up trying to find a station and switched it off.

"So where are you headed on this trip of yours?" he asked as we steered towards Portree, the main city on the island.

I told him a bit about my plans - that I was hoping to cover all of Britain and Ireland, as well as Europe, over the next few months. My next stop, however, was Belfast.

"Belfast?" his voice sharpened.

"Yes, I've got an interview with a peace group there. It's the start of the peace talks this Monday. All the sides are getting together to talk at Stormont. It's quite the event."

"Yes. I know."

We settled into an uneasy quiet. The sign for Portree flashed up ahead and we took a side road in order to skirt the city. I began to pick anxiously at a loose thread on my backpack, remembering headlines about murdered hitchhikers.

"I was there," he said suddenly.

We were headed into the heart of Skye, the unpopulated ghostly landscape of the Cuillins, the dark, bare hills that form the geographical centre of the island.

"There? You mean Belfast?"

"Yes."

"When?"

Mark glanced out at the side of the road. An empty crofter's cottage stood decaying in a field. "The early seventies. At the start of the troubles. I was in the Army, joined up when I was sixteen."

"Really?" I said, staring out at the deserted fields beside the road. There was an eerie desolation to the landscape, no houses, no people. I glanced in the mirror and was glad to see two cars behind us.

"Are you Catholic?" Mark asked suddenly.

I gave him a surprised look. "No."

He made an awkward twirling gesture with a finger towards my hair. "It's your red hair. I'm sorry, I shouldn't have asked. You just learn to spot things like that."

"Would it have mattered?"

"No, not at all," he stuttered out. "It's just that you're going to have to watch out for that when you're over there."

"Watch out for what? That people may think I'm Catholic?"

"Yes," he answered simply.

"Why, will it make me a target? Is that what British soldiers look for, the colour of your hair?"

Mark turned to look at me and I could see a mixture of anger and confusion in his small blue eyes. "Look, we didn't pick on the

Catholics. We went in to help them. Everybody forgets that. I remember women and kids in the Falls Road coming up to tell me how happy they were that I had come to protect them."

"How long did that last?"

"Until the killing really started. Then everyone hated us."

I glanced again in the side mirror, a chill prickling the backs of my arms at his casual tone. "How old were you?"

"Nineteen."

"Nineteen years old and in the middle of a war zone. That's ridiculous."

He shook his head no. "Not really. I'd been on my own for three years. Been around the world. I guess I felt I could handle anything."

"Even Belfast?" I couldn't keep the doubt from my voice.

"Yes, even Belfast." Mark smiled his Irish boxer's smile. All he needed was a broken nose and a North Dublin accent. "Stupid, huh?"

I said nothing.

"But you know," he pressed on, "it wasn't that bad at the beginning. And then when it got bad, it just became a part of life. You never really knew how bad it was until you went home on leave and saw how the rest of the world lived."

I hesitated. "How bad was it?"

Mark paused, and then shook his head firmly no. "I can't tell you about that."

"Why? I'm going to be there in a few days, talking to these people. You said yourself that people are going to mistake me for being Irish."

"I don't think it's right for me to talk about those kind of things with you," he said with a firmness that had an undertone of chivalry.

"That's ridiculous," I said heatedly. "Don't treat me like a weak woman. I can handle it."

Mark stared out at the strip of tarmac that was winding us through the desolate mountains, his lips twisting into a bitter smile. "Well, if you can handle it, Kim, you're a better man than I am." He turned to look at me, and the pain etched on his face mocked my assertions of strength. "They killed one of my best mates with piano wire. Sliced his head off. I was in the convoy behind him. Saw it all."

"The IRA?"

Mark laughed. "No, the kids. That wasn't even big time terrorism. That was what the children did for a bit of fun after school. Tied a string of piano wire across the street from the lamposts, just at the height where soldiers stand up in the back of the land rovers. It hits you as you drive by," he slapped himself with a karate chop against his adam's apple, "and slices your head off."

I gripped the strap of my knapsack so that it cut into my hand. "That must have been terrible."

"Was it terrible? I don't know. Maybe he got off easy."

I looked over at his hands. They were holding the steering wheel so tightly I could see the white bones of his knuckles showing through the skin.

"That's when they took me off infantry duty. Put me on as a paramedic, but it got worse. I didn't see the occasional killing. I saw it every night. Do you know what a bomb does to the human body? You don't even know who or what it is anymore. Sometimes you can't even tell the sex."

He had shifted forward in his seat, his hands pulling his body to the steering wheel as if the words were pummelling their way out of him. I glanced nervously behind us. The road was empty.

"They never let up. You never knew what was going to happen. Every step, every breath. You never knew. They called me Blondie," he turned and smiled at me with an almost comic fondness, "the IRA had a nickname for most of the soldiers. They'd leave notes for you. Just to let you know that they could enter the barracks if they wanted, or your pub." He paused for breath and examined the countryside as if it held some kind of answer for him. "Is this what you wanted to hear, Kim?"

I didn't answer. "How did you bear it?"

He shrugged. "I just did. You lived till you could go home on leave, or you prayed for another posting. I went home on leave once. There was a letter waiting there for me. 'Hi, Blondie,' it said, 'have a good vacation. We'll be looking forward to seeing you when you get back.'" He laughed, a sharp, humourless cackle, and I felt my stomach roll over with a combination of fear and disgust.

"But you survived," I said.

Mark glanced at me briefly before returning his attention to the road. "I came home."

"Left the army?"

"Yes. I got this position with the Ministry of Defense. It's alright."

"Married?"

He shook his head no. "Who would sleep with me? I can't get through the night without a bad dream. My pyjamas are soaked through by three o' clock in the morning." I felt a twinge of embarrassment at his brutal honesty. "It's because I just can't get it out of my head, you know? The sounds, the smell. It's trapped in there. Everything. That smell," I felt another flush of fear at the almost gleeful expression spread across his face, "right after a bomb blast. Burning flesh. It seeps into your nose, into your clothes, into ..."

"Stop it!" I shouted.

The car came to a jolting brake as a stop sign loomed up at a crossroad.

"I'm sorry." Mark pressed his face forward into the steering wheel, breathing heavily. "I'm sorry."

He straightened up and shakily wiped the sweat from his forehead. I carefully examined the black plastic knobs on the car radio.

"It's alright," I said, without looking at him. "I understand."

The car slowly started to move forward and we turned onto the coast road, leaving the dark mystery of the mountains behind us.

We changed the subject and talked about his new life in Lancashire. He told me about his ham radio hobby and his work with the legion and wounded vets. He seemed to envy them their physical scars, more visible and perhaps less painful than his own. He pulled a faded newspaper clipping from his wallet that showed him being awarded a medal by the queen. I told him about my family in Vancouver, and my hopes for a new column when I returned home.

We never mentioned Northern Ireland again.

Two hours later, we eased onto the open car ferry that sails across the narrow inlet from Skye to the Kyle of Lochalsh on the mainland. "I'm driving south. You're welcome to come if you want," Mark offered.

The flat car ferry chugged across the icy blue waters. Was there an unspoken invitation in his voice? A short respite from the memories, perhaps, or just a little warmth and comfort?

"No, thanks, Mark. I'll take the train."

He nodded with a phlegmatic acceptance, probably not realizing that he deserved more than my pity. Much more.

The white car rolled off the ferry and into the small town of Kyle of Lochalsh. We pulled to a stop beside a little tearoom, carefully avoiding the flow of tourists boarding a bus bound for Skye.

"Thanks again, Mark." I reached forward and kissed him quickly on the cheek before darting across the road and into the tearoom.

I didn't watch as he pulled away. Behind me I could hear a family quarrelling over whether their young son could finish the hamburger he wanted to order. A saucy, young waitress took my order for tea and scones and then disappeared into the kitchen.

I bent my head into my hands and began to cry.

vi Belfast: the prospects for peace ❖❖❖❖

Belfast was a tense city in the days preceding the peace talks. It presented itself as a paradox, a bizarre mixture of great warmth and a coldness that could frost your bones. The shops were shuttered, as were the faces of many of the citizens as they bustled in drab groups along the streets. But, like a flower in the snow, unexpected kindness and humour blossomed in the most unexpected places - from a song and a pint in the pub to an impromptu walking tour given by a retired postman.

I arrived at York station on a late Sunday afternoon, the grey, cold sky scudded with clouds. The group of people off the boat train from Larne huddled together like damp sheep awaiting the bus into the centre of the city. I decided to walk over and buy a newspaper.

"Which is your best paper?" I asked jokingly.

The newsagent, an older man with a fringe of grey hair on his head and a waxy coin pouch tied around his ample waist, turned to his son and poked him. "Best paper. That's a bit of a joke, isn't it?"

We all laughed and he pointed to a paper which lacked a "royals in midst of breakup" headline. "Try that one, Luv. Where are you from?"

I handed him some change. "Canada."

He looked surprised. "Canada? What are you doing here?"

I paused, as I wasn't sure I should bandy around my reason for being in Belfast. "I'm a journalist."

A defensive frown passed over the features of both father and son as my bus pulled up to the curb.

"Tell them in Canada that we're not all murderers here!" the father shouted after me as I hurried onto the bus.

I ignored the questioning stare of the bus driver as I fished out my fare and found myself a window seat.

The city itself did not look any different from anything I had seen in England. It had the same utilitarian Britishness to its architecture, the drab brick row housing that was so popular in the post-war era. I settled back in my seat. What was all the fuss about? This was just like England.

The bus came to a stop at a red light. An army Landrover pulled up beside us, two young soldiers armed with rifles standing in the back. Their faces were level with mine, their rifles pointing predatorily from their hands. They couldn't have been much out of their teens, their skin unlined and with the baby softness of minimal shaving. I was still staring at them when one of the soldiers swiveled his head towards me.

I felt a chill thud of fear land at the base of my stomach. His eyes were utterly devoid of emotion and so cold they could have been chipped from ice. What was more disturbing was that they didn't deviate from my face, which was only a few inches away. These eyes did not leer or politely glance away: these eyes controlled. Coming from a safe, suburban world, I had never experienced anything like it before.

I didn't look away, stubbornness or perhaps some terrible magnetic fascination held me there. I studied his face, the rounded curves of it, and the crinkly pale creases etched into the collar of his army fatigues. I wondered if he had ever made love to a woman, and what a sad world it would be if this gun was his introduction to manhood.

The light changed and the bus rolled forward. The Landrover gathered speed and passed us, the soldier turning his gaze once again to the enemy around him.

I was glad to reach the comparative safety of the hostel. A gangly, dark-haired man sat behind the entrance desk. He greeted my arrival with a languorous wave of a thin hand.

"Hello," he said in a soft twang.

Another Australian. I had come to Europe and all I seemed to meet were Australians.

"Hi. I'd like a bed for tonight."

"Sure," he pulled out a receipt to sign me in and produced a map of Belfast at the same time. "I suppose you want to know where the action is?"

I laughed. "Do I?"

He paused from his prepared recitation and looked up at me in surprise. "Don't you?"

"I guess so, though it isn't uppermost in my mind right now. I take it most of the people you get here are looking for some trouble?"

"Yeah, some. It's kind of a low-cost, thrill seeking experience. They're on their way to Dublin, so they think they'll come and see if they can survive Belfast first."

"No tourists?"

He shrugged his shoulders. "A few, but the serious tourists are usually headed up North and just spend the night here on the way. Is that what you're doing?"

"No, I'm going to be here for several days," I hedged.

His smile deepened. "Looking for a bit of trouble?"

I shook my head no. "Some understanding."

I met Phil, the informative warden, again after dinner. We sat in the dining room and fussed over an unsolvable crossword puzzle in one of the Sunday papers, laughing over our mutual stupidity. He was a philosophy graduate from Melbourne travelling the world looking for new experiences to be philosophic about. A year younger than me, he had arrived at the Belfast Youth Hostel and to both his and everyone else's surprise, stayed. His assistant, Rhonda, was a red-headed student from Seattle with an engaging sense of humour and a welcome taste for adventure.

I had not intended to discuss my reasons for visiting Belfast but, as our crossword puzzle session lengthened into an early morning chat complete with half a bottle of brandy, it became impossible to keep it secret. Phil knew of the group I was to interview, the Peace People, but was cautious about talking politics.

"Be careful who you talk to about this," he cautioned me over our fifth brandy. By now we had progressed from polite chit chat to intimate secrets. "Everybody in Belfast always seems to be talking about politics," he lisped drunkenly. "But you'll notice, they're always talking to someone who agrees with them."

I didn't need the brain-clearing blast of brandy fumes to get his point.

The next morning I awoke with a head cold and a hangover, not the most pleasant mixture for facing a new day in stressed-out Belfast. The morning papers were filled with details of the talks and the possibilties for peace. I hoped my interview with the chairperson of the Peace People, the most prestigious peace group in Northern Ireland, would be as optimistic.

The Peace People's offices were downtown so I caught a taxi from the hostel. The red brick house, a rambling two storey building, looked as if it had once been home to a large family. I knocked on the door and then entered a large room that must have been the parlour of the home. It was now the front office. Bits of paper fluttered everywhere while people, old and young, bustled among the desks and chairs.

A red-headed woman sat behind one of the desks, speaking on the telephone. She gestured me towards her, covering the mouthpiece with one hand. "I'll be with you in a minute."

I nodded yes and turned to meet the curious smiles of the volunteers in the room. There was a round of friendly good mornings.

With a final comment into the receiver, the red headed woman put the phone down. She looked up at me with good-humoured irritation and turned to a woman beside her.

"Sarah, could you take this journalist," she focused her eyes on my face, "It's Kim, isn't it? Yes, could you take Kim to one of the back rooms. I'll do the interview there. Oh, and bring her a cup of tea or something." She turned her attention back to her desk.

I found myself being led along a narrow corridor to a small room. I was left there on a folding chair with a cup of hot tea. Five minutes later, the red-headed woman strode into the room. With a forceful handshake, she introduced herself.

"I'm Ann McCann. Sorry about the delay. I'm afraid you've caught us at a very busy time, with the peace talks and all."

She sat herself down, her slim frame and pretty cotton dress quite a contrast to her tough demeanour.

"Well, I'll get right to the point then." I switched on my tape recorder and rummaged through my notes. "What do you think will be the outcome of the peace talks? Do they have a chance?"

McCann shrugged her shoulders and sipped at a cup of tea that had been brought in for her. "There's always a chance. At least we're talking, that's better than killing one another."

"How did you get involved with the Peace People?"

"I joined just after Mairead and Betty, the two women who formed the Peace People, won the Nobel Peace Prize. About 1977."

"Why?"

She took another sip of tea and appeared to be remembering something.

"It seemed then that we, the average people here, could actually change things. There was a great deal of hope, but maybe too much expectation of what the Peace People could achieve. It's a bit like the peace talks now. It's only a start."

"Nothing more?"

Ann smiled, hinting at an ironic sense of humour. "Well, the British press is treating these talks like they are the only chance for peace. People in Northern Ireland are under no such illusions. The average citizen here will say that it's good if these talks take place, but there's a lot more to be done before there's going to be peace."

I shifted forward on the folding seat, juggling my notes and the cup of tea. "But when the movement first started, you really believed you could bring about a speedy end to the violence?"

"Oh yes. We'd get fifty thousand people out for our rallies. But peace means different things to different people. We didn't have the wonderful reconciliation we hoped for, but things have improved. A lot of the old bigotries and prejudices have broken down. We've got integrated education now, although the numbers are still quite small. Our church leaders have come together to agree on a common curriculum for religious education in the schools."

"Did you grow up in Belfast?"

"Yes, although I did leave for ten years to live in Africa with my husband. I live in Andersonstown. Most Protestants wouldn't dream of driving through it, it'd be like going through West Beirut." She smiled her bittersweet smile again. "When I was growing up, I didn't even know what a Protestant looked like. I remember someone telling me that there was a Protestant girl on our street, so we detoured on the way to school to see whether she looked the same as us."

"You mentioned that you left Northern Ireland for ten years. Why did you come back?"

Her features hardened and I sensed something long tamped down rise up inside her. "My younger brother was killed at the start of the tit-for-tat shootings. He was nineteen, just coming back from a disco. I came back from Africa for the funeral." She paused again. "Sometimes you lose hope. I mean, just think about it. What do you do to bring about peace? Sometimes you're at a loss as to what has to be done to tackle these problems."

I waited for her to continue, but she turned her attention back to her cup of tea.

"And yet you're still fighting for peace. With so much suffering on both sides, is peace really possible?"

She smiled again. It was a smile that said I have been asked that question a thousand times, and I may never really know the answer.

"It would be very difficult to find anyone here who hasn't been touched by the troubles, that's true. Everyone's suffered. Both Catholic and Protestant. Perhaps that's the answer. Maybe we'll have to reach the point where everyone's suffered so much that no one lets the suffering continue."

The small room was too dark to take photographs for the column so we stepped out onto the back patio of the house. A high cement wall enclosed the yard. As I focused the camera, Ann kept inching to the left. I did not realize until later that she was trying to draw the camera away from the wall, the top of which was embedded with chunks of broken glass to discourage "visitors".

I left the Peace People's office and headed uptown to meet Rhonda, the assistant warden, and Margaret, another hosteller. Over a pint the previous night, they had asked if they could join me as I ventured in to take some photos of what Phil called "the action" of West Belfast.

I met them on the Falls Road, the street that is synonymous with the bloody sectarian riots of two decades ago. The Falls, a Catholic area, rests beside Shankill, a Protestant community. A barbed-wire-topped wall and strict security forces keep an uneasy peace between the two. Except for the number of big black cabs trundling along its length, however, the Falls Road was indistinguishable from any other part of the city.

We turned and headed east along the road, hunting for wall murals. These murals ranged from simply coloured slogans to dramatic representations of Republican heroes. Not graffiti, they were instead a kind of art as silent protest. We wandered along the rows of drab shops, looking for the tell-tale whitewash smears on the end of buildings.

"I think this is where you cross over into Shankill," said Rhonda as we came to a stop by a side street.

"Okay, let's go here then," I said and turned left into the narrow road.

The road angled sharply to the right on a blind corner, and we turned unthinkingly into it. Suddenly we were in the middle of a set from a Cold War film. A huge barricade, lined with zebra stripes, stood across the road. Cement blocks zig-zagged in front of it to stop any vehicles from trying to speed through the barricade.

Foolishly relaxed by our uneventful tour of the Falls, I continued to walk forward towards the crossing. Rhonda and Margaret slowed down and slipped into step behind me. A wooden guard hut stood beside the barricade and an armoured Landrover with two soldiers in it was parked down the lane. A soldier standing in front of the hut motioned with his machine gun for me to stop.

"You want to go in here?" he sneered, with a heavy dose of sarcasm.

I didn't answer at first because I was concentrating on his gun. I had never seen a machine gun this close before. It looked fake, like some large plastic toy. Belfast's version of Toys R Us. I unconsciously raised my hand as if to touch it. Margaret grabbed my arm from behind and yanked it down.

I nodded my head yes in answer to his question.

"Where are you from?"

"I'm from Canada, and they're from the United States and Australia," I answered, still mesmerized by the gun.

His expression of disgust changed to one of surprise. "You're not from Belfast?"

"No," we answered in unison.

"What were you doing with the scum down there then?" He nodded his head towards the Falls.

I looked up from the gun into his face. He was older than the other soldiers I had seen, wrinkles scoring his forehead in thick lines, a luxurious bristling moustache proof of his testosterone levels.

"We wanted to see the Falls Road," I answered.

He gestured with his machine gun over his shoulder in the direction of the Landrover. "Well, you're better off over here. Safer than with the shit down there."

"May we go through?" I asked slowly, trying to control my anger.

"Yes, but be careful. You shouldn't be wandering around here like this."

We had started to walk past the barricades when Margaret grabbed my sleeve. "Look up there, behind us," she whispered.

The three of us turned around. Thin slits had been cut into the cement walls of a barbed-wired building beside the barricade. A gun was pointing out of one of the slits, trained on our backs. We turned and continued through into Shankill.

The soldier was right, if only in one thing. Shankill looked just like Britain, with nothing but block upon block of red brick housing estates.

After a quick tour around, Rhonda left to return to the hostel while Margaret and I headed for the Donegall Pass area, another hot spot.

We walked along Shaftesbury Avenue. and past the Royal Ulster Constabulary post into Donegall Pass. Margaret spotted a large, brightly-colored Ulster Defence Force mural, and I stepped in front of it to snap a picture. A young girl, brown pigtails flying, came running out of her neat front yard and began to jump angrily up and down in front of me, her tiny fingers trying to block the lens.

I lowered the camera. "Hi."

She looked at me with a cynicism that was frightening in one so young. She couldn't have been more than eight. "I wasn't trying to say hello," she sniffed and went running back up the street, "and you know it."

I turned to Margaret. "That's it. I've got the picture. Let's get out of here."

We started to walk up the street towards a bus stop. A security forces Landrover cruised by and Margaret and I instinctively slowed our steps. Our experience in Shankill had taught us to be wary of the army. The Landrover proceeded a half block further on before one of the soldiers standing up through the sentry hole in the vehicle pivoted sharply and slammed a hand on the top of the vehicle. The land rover screeched to a stop.

A man in his early twenties was walking alone along the sidewalk towards us. We watched in horror as the two soldiers raised their guns to firing position and pointed them at the side of his head. The young man did not stop walking, his eyes concentrating on Margaret and me on the sidewalk ahead of him.

The street was suddenly silent. We clearly heard the rustling movement of cotton fatigue jackets as hands shifted on triggers. I looked at Margaret, only to see on her face the same open-mouthed shock that must have been on my own.

The young man slowed, a partial step hovering in the air. He waited, as did we all, for the reverberation of a shot.

There was nothing.

He took one step forward, and then another, each time waiting for the click of the trigger hitting home. His eyes never left mine, as if I was somehow drawing him along the street towards us. The soldiers waited, guns trained on his back, until he had brushed past the two of us and then, with the now familiar slam of the fist on the roof, started off down the road again.

Margaret and I looked at each other. “They were going to shoot him,” I said, my voice cracking in disbelief.

“I know,” she said.

A bubble of hysteria broke in my throat and I began to laugh with loud whoops of released tension. Margaret joined in and we stood in the middle of the road, holding one another and laughing wildly like two escapees from an insane asylum.

A fitting finale for Belfast.

But it wasn't quite the end. The peace talks started on schedule and proceeded through several weeks of petty wrangling before dissolving in angry discord. I stayed in Belfast for several more days, drinking too much and spending too much time with Phil. After a week in Belfast, he told me that I would never leave. I had given him the one sure sign: like the citizens of this bizarre warm-hearted city, I no longer noticed when the security forces drove by.

I left the next morning.

vii the dublin diet: how to eat nothing and still gain weight ❖

I had cheated. Instead of waiting to arrive in Dublin before tasting my first drop of Guinness, I had downed several pints in Belfast. The Irish, I felt, would understand why a draft of Guinness was necessary to survive the turmoil of Belfast.

Guinness is an Irish tradition. This dark fluid, thick to the taste and topped with a white band of froth, has long lubricated the throats of the singers and storytellers of Dublin's pubs. Every Irish writer had his favourite watering hole. You can follow them through the heart of Dublin like a trail of empty Guinness bottles, from the only pub Yeats ever visited to Seamus Heaney's home away from home. The Irish Tourist Board even hands out brochures listing Dublin's literary pubs. I was hoping that some of this liquid inspiration would rub off on me as I surged forward on my trek, counting my pennies and struggling to keep up with my column deadlines.

While waiting to use the phone in the lobby of the Dublin Youth Hostel on my first day in town, I saw a familiar face bearing down on me. It was Tom.

"Hey! What a surprise! Great to see you again," Tom said as he dropped his bags by my feet. "How long have you been here?"

I felt my spirits lift with an unexpected flush of happiness. Tom looked the same as he had on Skye, perhaps a bit scruffier in a waterproof jacket and faded jeans.

"Just got in an hour ago."

We hovered in embarrassed silence, Tom looking at me with undisguised pleasure. Inspiration struck.

"I'm going out later for a drink with a girl who's staying in my room. Would you like to come?" I asked.

His smile widened, the tips of his grey-flecked moustache tilting up at the corners. "Yeah, that sounds great. Oh," the smile dimmed, "I've already asked someone to go out with me tonight."

"Oh." I felt a surprising sense of loss.

"It's not a date or anything," Tom reassured me and my spirits leapt. "We just met while waiting to check in here. She's sitting out by the entrance desk."

"Well then, why don't you ask her to come along with us?"

"Sure, that sounds good. Let's go."

The girl was waiting by the entrance desk, the rounded hump of a backpack leaning against her bent leg. She smiled broadly when she saw Tom enter the room and then her eyes shifted to me beside him. Her smile rearranged itself into a questioning frown. Needless to say, she was not impressed by the idea of changing her cozy evening alone with Tom for a night out with a group of strangers. With a disgusted sniff, she refused Tom's delicately rephrased offer and retired to sulk in private. I couldn't have been happier.

As this was my first night in Dublin, I had high hopes that it would be rowdy, bawdy, loud and lecherous, filled with all the characteristics that make Dubliners so inspiringly bold and irritatingly brash.

The three of us - Tom, myself, and my roommate Vanessa - headed off to our first pub, which turned out to be a swank wine bar with quiet booths and tiffany glass. The young man who brought us our drinks informed us in a bored tone that the karaoke was on for the next night. He obviously thought we had come to sing "Climb every Mountain" to a synthesized beat. We drank up and moved on to another recommended pub.

Situated just down from St. Stephens Green in the heart of the city, our next pub, O'Donoghue's, was clearly the place for us. For one thing, it was packed. Any pub that attracts that many people is either a good thing or offering free booze, and I already knew that no Dubliner would be foolish enough to offer free booze. We squeezed our way inside.

O'Donoghue's was once a spit and sawdust pub - a traditional working class pub where men would gather to drink, sing and, I suppose, spit. I could still see a few wisps of sawdust on the wooden floor, but now it was there only for the tourists. In one corner, a group of men clustered around a table, their fingers whirring over traditional instruments. Smoke swirled in thick whiffs in the air as we pushed our way towards the counter.

A row of barmen stood behind the bar, pouring and serving, working the spigots, effortlessly tossing foaming pints onto the counter. At the end of the bar, a man stood on a stool behind the counter, one heavy-booted foot on the bar itself. Like an auctioneer, he gathered orders for the bar and then shouted them back to the scurrying barmen.

Having been prepared earlier, I raised a hand and shouted: "Three pints!"

The man at the bar was stocky with thick blond hair waving off a ruddy, beer congested face. His eyes scanned the noisy crowd until they found mine. He hesitated, sensing a tourist gaffe in the making, and then shrugged his shoulders. "Three pints!" he screamed to a young barman and gestured me up to the bar with a long finger.

I counted out the large Irish pound notes and handed him the money. He smiled as I gently picked up the three pints of foaming Guinness and headed back through the crowd to Tom and Vanessa. I was quite pleased with myself. I had ordered the Irish way.

We squeezed our way through the narrow length of the pub, hoping to find a few square inches of breathing space. Everyone seemed to have their fingers wrapped around a glass of the frothy black liquid. Women sipped it daintily, dropping their heads to its creamy top, while men used it as some kind of intellectual battering ram, punctuating each conversational point with an emphatic wave of the glass. I tried to stay away from the more drunk and emotional conversationalists as we manoeuvered our way through the throng. There was a good chance of getting side-swiped by a liquid exclamation point.

Finally we reached the back of the pub and I felt a wonderful gush of fresh air from an open back door.

"Do you hear some music?" asked Vanessa as we hovered in a dim corner.

"I think it's coming from outside. Let's go have a look," said Tom.

The crowds had spilled out into the alley behind the pub. The air was cool and fresh, with an early evening dampness to it. Lamplit young people sat on apartment fire escapes, perched on wooden boxes, or leaned up against the moss-covered stone walls. In the middle of the alley, surrounded by a casual semi-circle of admirers, sat a group of young men. They were playing a variety of instruments: a couple of guitars, a tin whistle, and an old bodhran, or traditional flat drum. With their long hair and patched jeans, they looked like they should be in a rock band. Instead they produced beautiful Irish folk songs.

I looked around the circle of listeners, most of them in their late teens. These young people listened intently, with respect and admiration. No one hooted for the latest heavy metal hit.

A young American girl arrived to a welter of hugs and kisses. She was given a seat of honour with the group - an old whiskey crate - and began to sing a sweet, plaintive Celtic melody. Snatches of people in the crowd sang along. There was a rustle of applause as the song came to a close.

"Now we'll sing one from my country," she laughed in a soft American accent and whispered something to the flautist.

He nodded his head and began to play a simple version of "Amazing Grace". Her voice chimed in, high and pure, her round-cheeked face pointing up to the starry sky. The three of us drifted, light-headed, down the alley towards the road, her sweet voice following us towards St. Stephens Green.

I continued my in-depth Guinness investigation by heading to the Guinness factory a few days later. Located in a block-long strip of buildings near the Liffey River, the factory covers a huge chunk of downtown Dublin. It looked like a federal institution with its grey buildings and high security wall. Only the rich sour-sweet mash smell of brewing beer gave it away.

I arrived at the gate, only to be met by an armed security guard.

"I'm here to speak to your public relations person," I said.

The guard stirred himself from his seat and lazily walked over to me. "Name please," he stated flatly.

"My name?"

"No. The person you would like to speak to."

"I don't know. I was told to come to this gate and ask for the public relations person."

"You're a journalist?" he asked doubtfully.

"Yes."

"Wait here." He returned to his guard hut and made a long, involved telephone call. When he reappeared, he pointed me in the direction of one of the buildings.

Leonie Brennan, the anonymous public relations person, greeted me with an armful of press clippings and a pleasant grin. We sat down to talk and I bombarded her with all the myths I had heard about Ireland's famous beverage.

"It's true, at one time Guinness was made from the waters of the Liffey," she said and looked out towards the famous river that divides Dublin. It looked as if it had accumulated a fair amount of its garbage now too. "But now we have our own water resources outside of the city."

When I asked her about the health claims that are made for Guinness, that dying men on the battlefield have been revived by its taste, she laughed. "It's true. Hospitals give it to new mothers to help them keep up their strength. Like the slogan says: Guinness really is good for you. It's even a low-calorie drink, something that's very popular these days."

I bristled at this. "Guinness is low in calories?"

"Definitely. It's a much lighter drink than most people think."

My hand surreptitiously felt its way over my stomach. I had spent a good part of the last week working my way through Dublin's pubs, researching this story. In fact, a fair share of my eating funds had been used in order to keep me in Guinness. Despite my decreased food intake, I could still feel my stomach pressing against my pants with a watery bloatedness.

Low-calorie, my foot.

After my interview with Leonie, I toured the Hop Store and visited the museum, one of Dublin's biggest tourist attractions. After watching an explanation of the brewing process and a short film on the Guinness history of stout making, I arrived in the basement to taste my free sample. It tasted good, but somehow lacked the added flavour I enjoyed when sipping it in the leather-ensconced tackiness of a true Dublin pub.

Saturday was spent wandering the streets of Dublin. O'Connell Street was in the process of being transformed into a huge street fair, as an army of overall-clad men putting together rides with names like Octopus Twist and The Screamer.

Crowds thronged Grafton Street, the shopping epicenter of the city. Buskers played every kind of music from Irish folk to classical, while young girls plaited hair with brightly coloured cord. Huge crowds of Spanish language students congregated in front of McDonald's, eating their Big Macs and chattering away like Madridlenos rather than using the English language their parents had sent them to this Catholic country to learn.

And everywhere there was noise - people laughing and shouting, the thick Dublin accent clashing against my ears. My expectations of a land of pleasant leprechauns had taken a beating since I'd arrived in this city. People pushed and shoved, darted out into traffic with a daredevil's deftness, and swore at the slightest provocation.

I was not the only foreigner to find Dublin a culture shock. While walking along the street one day with a young woman I'd met at the hostel, we found ourselves being constantly jostled by passing pedestrians.

"I don't believe this," she said angrily to me after she had been knocked off the sidewalk for the third time. "Doesn't anybody here say excuse me? Why does everybody expect me to move for them?" She gritted her teeth in determination and stared down the sidewalk at a couple of teenage girls walking towards us. I felt a confrontation coming on. "I'm not moving for them. That's it. Somebody is going to have to move for me!"

We continued on a direct course for the girls. It reminded me of childhood games of chicken, waiting anxiously to see who would balk first. Judging by the glint in the eye of my hostel aquaintance, it was going to have to be the young Dublin girl.

The girl glanced up, noticed us coming, and then turned to speak to her friend. She did not move out of the way. Neither did we.

They collided head on, with a concussion that threw them both back onto the sidewalk. As far as my fellow hosteller was concerned, this was all the proof she needed that Dublin was the worst city on Earth. She shouted it in more colourful terms than this as she scrambled up from the pavement. The teenager was helped up by her friend and added some piquant observations of her own on the subject of tourists and other such vermin. The swearing, I'm sure, could be heard for blocks.

I eventually learned to like Dublin. I, too, attempted suicide when crossing the road, and even began to push back in queues rather than politely take it. Which was just as well, for no one ever did get out of my way on the sidewalk.

My final night in Dublin arrived in concert with the end of the summer fair. Tom and I and a group from the hostel had decided to take a last sentimental pub tour before heading off to see the fireworks. After a final pint at our favourite pub, we trooped to the river's edge. The lit bridges which cross the river were coated with people. Behind us, drunken youths climbed up Parnell's statue and hung from his shoulders, singing ridiculous ditties. Green and red splashes lit up the evening sky in electrical bursts.

Light-headed from too much Guinness, I sloppily looked over at Vanessa, who was busily munching her way through her newest passion, Dunkin' Donuts, and saw that Tom was watching me. He was smiling strangely.

Another blast of fireworks went off, tinting our skin a pale red, and I shrieked at the loud bang, forgetting immediately what I had seen for an instant in his eyes.

viii the last Irish storyteller ❖❖❖❖❖❖

And Father John, before he's gone, will bless the house and all!"

I hummed as I picked up my bags and jumped off the Tralee train onto the trellised station platform.

I was bound for the Dingle Peninsula. I have always been fascinated with the magic of the *seanachais*, or Irish storytellers, and desperately wanted to meet and interview such a person. Such traditions, I realized, were dying off faster than animals on the endangered species list.

"How grand it feels, to kick your heels, and join in the fun of the jigs and reels," I sang softly, my voice rising as I stepped out into the lane in front of the station. "It's Christmas in Killarney!" I came to a gulping stop as I noticed a woman waving to me from a small car. I walked over, wondering if she was going to complain about my singing or merely the unseasonal choice of song.

"Excuse me," she said as I reached the open window, her voice conveying both confidence and a note of shyness, "but I'm afraid I overheard you talking to that gentleman on the train. I was wondering if you'd like a lift in to Dingle?"

I forgot my musical impropriety and almost did a jig on the spot. "Yes, I'd love it. Thank you."

She popped open the side door and I clambered in.

"My name is Eileen," she said as we revved up and shot out of the station parking lot. I introduced myself and she nodded, apparently unashamed that she had eavesdropped on my conversation with a fellow Canadian on the train. "Yes, I know. Are you here about Funghie or is it the stars you're after?"

So much for the shyness. It had burnt away like an early morning Irish mist.

"Neither really. Who is Funghie and which stars are you talking about?"

She laughed and explained that the major attractions at present in Dingle were Funghie, the wild dolphin who lived in the bay, and the horde of American film stars who were helicoptering in and out of town checking out locations for a film.

I sucked in a mouthful of air as we narrowly avoided rearranging the wardrobe of a young woman who was walking along the side of the road. Eileen didn't even blink, only picked up speed and began to drive even faster around the hairpin curves.

"No, I'm actually here to see if I can find an Irish storyteller," I said, biting the inside of my lip as we whizzed around another bend.

Eileen turned and looked at me, a dangerous thing to do with her driving skills. "An Irish storyteller. And why would you be wanting that?"

I explained that I was writing a number of columns about the culture and the people of the different places I was visiting. To expand on this, I told her about being caught by soldiers while attempting to go to the bathroom at the Trooping of the Colour.

She laughed when I concluded the story, but there was a sharp edge to her words. "Ahh, I know why the soldiers went after you." She nodded her thin nose towards my short red hair. "They thought you were IRA."

My laughter died in my throat. It was the first time I had heard politics mentioned in the South.

Eileen was the head sister at the hospital in Dingle. She was in her forties, with a trim figure and a shock of short red hair. She had grown up in Dingle, and apart from some years doing medical missionary work, had never left. She had the brisk, bossy manner of a nurse and treated me like a young, rather irresponsible patient.

"Where are you staying?" she asked as we rounded a green bend in the road and began to dip down into the luscious, postcard pretty town of Dingle.

"I don't know. A bed and breakfast somewhere, I suppose," I answered absently. I was concentrating on the beautiful scenery around us. I had thought Britain was green, but nothing compared to this drenched, glimmering richness. In this matriarchal country, even the earth seemed feminine and fertile. Moisture hung in sheets in the air. When the sun was out, I could see a shimmering humidity in the distance.

"Well, if it's an Irish storyteller you're looking for, I'll drop you at the Collins'. Their son studies Irish history at school. They're good people," she added as we slowed down to enter the town.

We pulled up in front of a small white cottage. A painted sign hung on the quaint black cast iron gate. Kirrarry, it read.

"I'll tell Moira that you're here," Eileen called enigmatically back to me as she drove off up the road.

Mr. Collins, the chief constable of Dingle, answered the door. He showed me to a bedroom, commenting nervously all the while on how his wife usually handled these things. She was, he added as I dropped my bags, working at the polling station in town today.

I was warming myself in front of their turf fire half an hour later when the front door opened with a bang and I heard a shout in the hall.

"So where's our visiting journalist?"

The door opened into the parlour and a chubby, red-cheeked woman appeared, a scarf draped artistically over her shoulder. "Hello,

Dearie. And how are you keeping? Did my husband look after you alright?"

This was Moira. She bustled into the room and plopped onto a cushioned seat beside me. Eileen, it appeared, had proceeded from Kirrarry to the polling station. By teatime, everyone in Dingle knew everything there was to know about me save for the results of my last dental checkup and the sex of my cat.

"So tell me all about yourself," Moira started off and settled back into the cushions for a long chat.

Fifteen minutes later, we were still discussing everything from employment opportunities in Canada to my religious beliefs. She seemed deeply interested in my faith. The house was dotted with religious pictures, which was not unusual in Ireland. Moira's quizzing, however, did not seem to carry with it any desire to convert me, but rather an honest curiousity about how the other half lived. To change the subject, I asked her about the possibility of finding an Irish storyteller.

"You're wanting a storyteller?" she asked, surprised.

"Yes, I am," I nodded.

"Michael? Will you come in here?" A young man appeared in the doorway, dressed in jeans and a t-shirt.

"Yes, Mother. What is it?"

"This young lady here," Moira nodded in my direction, "is looking for an Irish storyteller. Do you think Bab Feritear might speak with her?"

Michael wandered into the parlour and squatted down on the arm of a chair. He nodded his head musingly. "I don't know. I suppose she would. But you know, she doesn't speak English well."

"Yes, but she speaks it well enough, don't you think?" Moira turned to me. "Michael has just finished his degree in Irish at the university. He worked with Bab in his last year there. She lives in Dunquin, at the end of the peninsula by the Blasket Islands."

"She's a grand woman," Michael chipped in. "Spent her entire life there. She even knew Peg Sayers."

"Will she speak with me?"

Michael paused, and then a wide smile split his boyish face. "I think so. Just tell her I've sent you." He reached for a slip of paper and scribbled a map. "This is how to get to Dunquin. You can go there in the morning."

"Is there a bus? I'm afraid I don't have a car."

Both mother and son laughed.

"You don't need a car here. Just hitch," said Michael.

I shook my head no, feeling embarrassingly conservative. "I don't like hitching."

Moira's eyebrows turned up in a quizzical slant. "Don't people hitch in Canada?"

"No. It's too dangerous. You never know who's going to pick you up. It's illegal anyway."

Moira laughed, her red cheeks pushing upwards in a fleshy thrust. "Well, it's illegal here too. But that's never stopped anyone from doing it."

On that typically Irish note, I excused myself and headed out to explore the town. I followed the main street down towards the waterfront, wandering past the brand new mini-market, the tottering pubs with their peeling paint, and the handful of dark but expensive tourist restaurants.

I had just reached the main intersection, which had the only stop sign in town, when a car shot past me. There was a loud screech of brakes, and then the car began to reverse in my direction. It pulled level with me as the back window was rolled down.

"Kim! I don't believe it's you!" two high-pitched Australian voices yelled out happily.

It was Nat and Van. Ever since Glasgow, I had been hoping to meet up with my two Australian friends. I had missed them in Dublin by only a few days, and had sadly picked up their goodbye note from my mail stop. Our only other chance for a meeting had been planned for my final stop in Ireland, the southern city of Cork.

"Come on, Kim. Jump in!"

I dazedly clambered into the back of the car. There were hugs all around. In the frenzy of hands and arms clutching me, Nat spotted a masculine pair glazed with red hair.

"Stephen, don't be ridiculous," she said and with a coquettish slap pushed him back into the front seat.

Stephen, who was driving the car, pulled his hand back with a good-natured grin. He looked to be in his early twenties, with short hair and thick glasses. In the passenger seat, a heavier young man leered through the gap at Van.

"This is Stephen, Kim," Nat introduced me and I found myself, squished in between Nat and Van, nodding my head in greeting. "And this is Mark."

The weighty young man grinned. His eyes slipped from me to Van with the kind of hungry stare a cat gives a full bowl of catnip.

It seemed that Nat and Van, unable to find work, had decided to hitchhike down to the South before returning to England. Somewhere south of Galway, they had been picked up by Stephen and Mark. Instead of dropping them in their home town of Tralee, the two young men had decided to drive them all the way to Dingle.

"So what on earth are you doing here?" Nat asked as we pulled into the centre of town.

I told them about my endeavours to find an Irish storyteller, and that I was off to the end of the peninsula to speak to someone in the morning.

"Are you free this evening?" Van asked.

I nodded my head yes.

"Well, why don't you come out for a drink with us? You know a good pub, don't you, Mark?"

Stephen and Mark spoke softly for a moment to one another before naming an old pub in the centre of town. We made plans to meet there later that evening.

After a dinner out, I returned to Kirrarry to change for the evening. Despite my attempts to leave the house quietly, Moira caught me in the hall and cajoled me into the parlour.

"You must sing a song for me before you go," she said. "It's traditional."

Thinking this was a foxy Irish way of pulling a tourist's leg, I refused. But Moira stood her ground, and I finally gave in. My voice started off weak, but gained strength until the rousing tones of a gospel number rang throughout the house. Instead of giggles, my performance was greeted with serious attention. Moira close her eyes and gently slapped her thigh in rhythm to the music. When I finished, she opened her eyes and applauded.

"Is that the kind of song you sing in your church?"

"Sometimes," I hedged, not wanting to be brought back to the subject of religion again. Sensing a good chance for escape, I left her sitting in the parlour, musing on the strangeness of Protestant hymns.

I arrived at the pub at eight. It consisted of a single large room with a bare wood floor and round chipped tables which smelled of stale beer and aging wood. The walls seemed to sag with the weight of their existence, the fading memorabilia posted there slowly pulling them earthward. Light glinted weakly through narrow windows.

I recognized my group sitting near an huge old fireplace coated with the black ash of long-dead fires. I was half-way across the room before I realized there were two extra seats at the table, one of them already filled.

"Kim," Stephen called out boozily. "We've been waiting for you." Four heads swiveled to greet me. Stephen stood up and gave me a hearty hug. Rather too hearty, I felt, for someone I barely knew. "And here's Neil. We all went to school together."

Neil shuffled shyly to his feet. He was dark, the typical Western Irish descendants of Irish women and Spanish explorers, and hefty with a pleasant, rather dim expression. He was dressed in a formal shirt and tie. I wore a casual t-shirt and short skirt.

I shook his damp hand and sat down in my seat, shooting daggers at both Nat and Van. Van gave me a compassionate wink.

"We gave Neil a call before dinner. Thought he might like to come out for a drink," Stephen added.

And make us an even group, I added silently.

However irritated I was, I couldn't deny that Neil was a sweet young man. He was rather slow, his naivete making him the perfect butt for the jokes of the other young men, especially Mark.

"Pretty nice tie there, Neil," Mark jeered, and made a grab for the end. Neil pulled away from him, blushing. "Trying to impress someone, are we?" Mark continued, intent on squeezing out every last drop of pleasure from Neil's discomfiture.

"I think it's a nice tie," I said angrily.

"Yeah, I like a man in a tie," Van added. "I think it looks good on him."

Mark looked from me to Neil, a leacherous grin spreading across his face. It was not difficult to figure out what he was thinking.

Unfortunately, it looked as if Neil agreed with Mark's interpretation of my actions. As the night progressed, Guinness after Guinness kept magically appearing before me.

"Whoooo keeps buying me thish Guinness?" I lisped drunkenly. I looked at the growing number of dirty glasses stacking up on our table. It looked like the dripping remnants of an Octoberfest party.

Neil shyly patted me on the arm. "Don't worry about it, Kim. Drink up."

But his attempts to impress me with an unlimited supply of Guinness were useless. I had already, I realized as I attempted to stand up and make my way to the toilet, had enough.

I don't remember when I started to sing Beach Boys songs, but it was some time after I had staggered my way back from the ancient bathroom. The pub was packed with local citizens, and a haze of smoke drifted like a flat cumulus cloud above us. Two men and a young girl of about ten had taken up positions against one wall, playing softly on two drums and an accordion.

Our table looked like a frat party run amok - empty glasses nestling together, tipping haphazardly on to other glasses. Full pints of Guinness waited on the tabletop to be drunk, the white foam slipping down the mouths of the glasses into a creamy mush.

"Surfin' City USA," I belted out. Nat and Van joined in. I think I felt, somewhere in the back of my boozy brain, that I was representing the West Coast beach culture I had grown up in. Or maybe I just couldn't remember the words to any other songs.

"Surf's up, here we go," we sang lustily, eyes closed, heads back.

"Kim." I felt a hand on my shoulder. "Kim," the voice persisted.

I opened my eyes and saw Stephen standing beside me. I glanced dizzily around the room and realized that everyone else was standing too.

"Kim, stand up." Stephen reached underneath my arms and dragged me unsteadily to my feet.

"Whhaaat issh it?"

"It's the national anthem."

My eyes focused on the tattered trio playing softly on their rag tag instruments. The young girl continued to beat on her drum, her eyes staring intently at the floor. I looked at the faces around me and saw eyes lit by a desperate fierceness.

I felt terrible, and it wasn't just the drink. I felt I had somehow cheapened this demonstration of national pride with my pop songs, and would have quietly walked out if I could. Well, maybe crawled out. The music came to a close, and the entire pub erupted in a single shout of "Up Kerry!"

"It's in support of the local football team," Stephen told me as we staggered out into the night air.

I shook my head in understanding and felt my brain bounce soggily in my skull. I wanted to say something, to apologize, but it was too late. It was time to go to bed.

The next morning my head felt like somebody had placed a tin bucket over it and was beating away with a club. I stared at my cooked breakfast of bacon, eggs and fried slice and felt my stomach juices boil up in revolt.

"Don't you like your fried mushrooms?" Moira asked.

I looked up to see her smiling mischeviously down at me. She must have heard me stagger in in the early hours. And if not that, she most definitely heard the well-meaning shouts of goodbye from my group. She knew I had the hangover from hell.

"Lovely. They're just lovely," I whispered.

Hitchhiking turned out to be much easier than I had expected. Within fifteen minutes, I was picked up by a mother and her young son. She proved how helpful Irish drivers can be by going out of her way to drop me in a good hitchiking spot for the remaining distance to Dunquin.

It wasn't long before another car slowed down and pulled onto the gravel verge ahead of me. I ran up to the open window.

"Hi. Where are you going?" An American voice drifted back to me.

A man of fifty was sitting in the driver's seat. His red hair and florid complexion gave him away as Irish in ancestry, his polo shirt and polyester pants marked him as an American tourist.

"Dunquin. Are you headed over there?"

He took a quick look at his map and then squinted up the road ahead of us. "I think so. Is it near Slea Head?"

"Just past it, I think."

"Oh well, jump in. We'll find it eventually." I eased myself into the passenger seat. "So you're a tourist too, are you?" he asked as we headed along the narrow road towards Slea Head at the end of the peninsula.

"Not really. I'm a journalist, here to interview a storyteller in Dunquin."

"Really? I'm in plastics."

He was from New Jersey, and had taken a few days off business in Dublin to rent a car and drive around Ireland. His name was Dan.

"Here's Slea Head," he said as we pulled up on a grassy patch beside the headland.

Even from the bottom, it looked beautiful - an emerald finger of land shooting out into the frothy Atlantic, the edge dusted with white sand beaches like snowy bites from a sour green apple. We climbed up the steep rocky path to the top. The sky was a cloudless blue and I felt as if I could reach out and touch the misty tip of Massachusetts a thousand miles in the distance.

The Blasket Islands, now uninhabited, sat in the bay beside us. Here fishermen had bobbed in ancient boats, telling the myths of land and sea. Peg Sayers had chronicled the life of these islands, rich with the whiffs of peat fires and homemade liquor. The countryside around me looked virtually unchanged. The green fields were dotted with an occasional white cottage, a stream of blue grey smoke winding its circuituous path skyward.

"Beautiful here, isn't it?" Dan commented as we stood snapping photos.

"Definitely."

We trekked back down to the bottom. Instead of heading back to the car, however, Dan veered towards a neighbouring field where we could see a man working. I hesitantly followed behind him, more out of a sense of politeness than curiousity.

"Good morning," he called out and, to my horror, stepped over the roped boundary and right into a furrowed field.

A man in dusty working clothes glanced up from where he was planting. He gazed at Dan, in his drip-dry stripes, and then looked pointedly back down at the tilled earth.

"Good morning," Dan persisted, his good humour undentable.

The man paused in his work and looked up with an utterly unwelcoming expression. "Good morning," he replied flatly and returned to his planting.

I watched with disbelief as Dan tramped unthinkingly over the neatly plowed furrows until he was looking down at the spot where the man was crouched, attempting to ignore him.

"What are you planting there? Potatoes?"

With a grumble that sounded like a mother bear greeting an unwanted intruder, the Irishman dusted off his hands and stood up. He leisurely examined Dan, from his jaunty golf cap down to his steadily sinking footwear.

"Marijuana," he answered simply.

I gulped in a laugh, and the farmer turned to look at me with a gleam of knowing humour in his eyes.

"Marijuana," Dan mused, and bent down to examine some of the earth. "How interesting."

It was obvious that Dan didn't get the joke, that he didn't know what marijuana was. I couldn't believe it. Neither could our Irish farmer, whose face was taut in a painful attempt to hold back a grin.

"Is that a cash crop around here?" I asked, trying to keep any levity out of my voice. "I thought people here preferred their Guinness and whiskey."

The Irishman allowed a tiny grin to spread across his face. "That's so. But marijuana adds a nice bit of variety."

Dan looked from me to the Irishman, a light of doubt beginnning to creep across his broad, placid features. "What is marijuana, Kim?"

"It's pot, Dan. You know, a drug. I'm afraid this man has been having you on. A practical joke."

The Irishman's face split into a wide grin and he released his pent up laughter in loud whoops. He didn't seem to care that Dan's cheeks had turned an angry shade of fuschia. In fact, he seemed inordinately pleased about the whole thing, as if he could hardly wait to tell everyone at the pub about how he had put one over on a gullible Yank.

"It's really potatoes," he said. "This is all a set for an American film. We're just setting up some gardens for them, so that they'll be grown by the time they start shooting."

We chatted for a few more minutes, but I could see that Dan wanted to go. His pride was hurt, and he wanted to remove himself from the scene as quickly as possible. As we drove off up the road towards Dunquin, I somehow doubted that this particular tale would make it into the round of stories he would tell about his trip to the old country.

Dan let me off with a brief goodbye in Dunquin, and I tactfully mentioned nothing about our encounter with Irish agriculture. He drove off in a hurry, hoping, I suppose, to shake the dust of Slea Head from his shoes.

A postman on a bicycle tottered past me, a leather bag flapping against his thigh.

"Excuse me," I called out.

He dropped his feet down and slowed to a dusty stop. "*Dia dhuit*," he greeted me in Gaelic.

"*Dia dhuit*. I'm looking for Bab Feirtear. Could you tell me where she lives?"

The postman, his knobby arthritic knees showing through his tattered trousers, turned his head to one side and examined me quizzically. With a pantomime gesture, he raised his hand up flat in the air and gestured me to stay, and then called to a handful of playing children. A young boy of eight came running over and there was a brief conversation in gaelic.

"What do you want?" the boy asked me in English.

"I'm looking for Bab Feirtear."

"She's in the last house on the street, the green one." The young boy bobbed his head in goodbye and returned to his football game.

I thanked the postman in gaelic and headed down the street. Old cottages lined one side of the narrow road. On the other side, green fields dipped down to the ocean. The Blaskets sat like imperturbable rock obelisks, Pagan statues from a dark, ancient time.

Bab Feirtear's house was made of old stone rimmed with green wood. I pushed through the wooden gate and up the stone steps to the front door. I knocked tentatively, unsure of what her reaction would be to an uninvited caller.

The door was finally opened by an elderly woman. She was short, with the stooped gait and thick trunk of someone who has laboured hard her entire life. Her hair was cut short and she had a pair of steel-rimmed spectacles perched on her nose.

"*Dia dhuit*."

"*Dia dhuit*," I answered. "My name is Kim Herdman. Michael Collins sent me."

Confusion wrinkled her seamed brow, but cleared at the sound of Michael's name. "Michael," she said in a voice that was quiet and raspy. "You know Michael?"

"Oh yes," I said, hedging. "I'm interested in writing about an Irish storyteller and he recommended I speak to you."

"Oh," she paused, and I could tell that she was wrestling with the idea. "But I don't speak the English well, you see."

"Don't worry. It'll be fine."

"Michael sent you," she murmured, more to herself than me, and with a sigh stepped out the front door. "We can sit here," she pointed to the steps, "to talk."

She settled herself on the sun-warmed stones, smoothing her heavy woollen skirt down towards her old-fashioned boots. A cur dog appeared with a growl and a bark from around the side of the house. She shooed him away in a loud flurry of Gaelic. He tucked his tail between his legs and sulked back to the garden.

We both laughed.

"He doesn't," she searched for the correct word, "bite. Just makes noise."

I clicked on the tape recorder, and she leaned away skittishly. "Would you prefer me to take notes? We don't have to use the tape recorder."

"No. It's my English. It's not good."

"You should hear my Gaelic." I stumbled my way through a few phrases of my quickly learned Irish.

A smile cracked its way through the fissures on her walnut brown face. Despite her seventy-odd years, her smile was sweet with the guilelessness of a child.

"Good." It sounded more like a germanic *gut*. "But you say it like this." She burred her way through the phrase with lilts and sounds that I could never reproduce. Her accent was not city Irish, but thicker and darker, untainted by soft English vowels.

"I suppose everyone around here used to speak Irish, didn't they?"

She nodded slowly. "Yes. The Irish isn't good now. Not good."

"But it used to be?"

She smiled and ducked her head with a Japanese timidity. If I wasn't careful, this interview was quickly going to degenerate into sign language.

"Tell me what life used to be like around here. Did everyone tell stories?"

She tucked her flat brown laced boots under her skirt and rocked gently on the step. "There was nothing else to do then. Nothing else. The old women had their own stories. The men had their stories and poems."

"And what were the stories about?" I prodded.

"They were about everything," she said simply, "about everything. They were about fairies, people who had died."

"Were they magical stories? About monsters and leprechauns?"

Bab wrinkled her nose at this and shook her head in polite disgust. "No, they were not. They were about your own people."

"Your own people? People in the village?"

"Yes, but who had died. Sometimes these people would come back in spirit form to ask you to pray for them."

Her manner implied that this was commonly accepted, this netherworld of spirits which existed in tandem with the village life of her childhood, and was neither unusual nor frightening. I continued with my simple questions, slowly building up a profile of her life.

Her childhood had been a difficult one. She had helped to raise a large family as well as look after an invalid grandfather. It was from him that she had learned her rich treasure store of Irish myths and stories.

"Our house was more like a school. My grandfather was blind and he had no other pastime than stories and poems."

"So you liked storytelling, even as a child?"

Once again, she wrinkled up her nose and laughed, as if I had made a joke. "That was for old women. I didn't want people to know

I could tell stories, then everyone would think I was old. I hid them, until I had my own children."

"And did they enjoy them?"

She shrugged her shoulders at the vagaries of her own children's taste. "Sometimes. Now I teach them to many children."

Bab told her stories on a weekly Gaelic radio show and also had a regular position speaking to children in the local school. Scholars from Dublin and America had already trekked out to her little green house to tape her stories for posterity.

The sounds of a group of schoolchildren singing a song in loud, discordant Gaelic came drifting down the road towards us.

"They're from the city, maybe Dublin," Bab said, and sat up taller to see the fifty or so children skipping along the road behind a teacher.

"*Dia dhuit*!"

One after the other, the children shouted the greeting as they spotted this new quarry to practise their recently learned Gaelic on. Bab laughed and said something to them loudly in Gaelic.

"Do they come here every summer to learn Irish?" I asked.

"Yes, and to see what life was like in the *gaeltacht*." Bab watched them as they trooped noisily down the road.

"*Gaeltacht*, you mean the Irish speaking regions of Ireland?"

"Yes, that's right."

"What will happen to the stories?" I asked, trying to drag her attention back to the interview. "Can the traditions survive?"

She shook her head. "They'll fade." She looked across the placid water to the Blaskets, once home to a thriving fishing community; now nothing but wind and ruins. "They will, I suppose."

Silence settled over us. Bab rocked happily on her step, pleased to be finished with the chore of speaking English. We listened to the buzzing of sun-drugged honeybees and the distant singing of children.

No translation was needed.

viv escape from kerry

The road sign said Waterville. Despite the reservations of the Bolognese couple who had given me a lift from Dingle, I insisted that this was the place. My guidebook had recommended Waterville as an idyllic stopover while touring the Ring of Kerry, a well touristed route best known for its scenic views of this lovely western county. Of course, it didn't look like much, obscured by the rain that had plagued us all morning, but Waterville was the one time home of Charlie Chaplin and a gem of an Irish village. Or so said the guidebook.

With an Italian *ciao* and a kiss on both cheeks, they motored off in their little rental car. The mist closed in around me. As I was contemplating the foolishness of my decision to stop here, an antiquated motorcycle came speeding up the muddy road. With a quizzical glance in my direction, the rider zipped past, liberally spraying my legs with muddy water.

I knew then that the Ring of Kerry was going to be an experience. Not necessarily a good one, but an experience nonetheless.

The Waterville Leisure Centre was constructed of blackened blocks inscribed with heavy Victorian stone work. It hovered over the beach like a large and imposing raven and was as empty and quiet as the village itself.

"Hello!" I shouted in the vault-like entrance hall. "Hello!"

It looked like an abandoned country manor house, with its winding staircase and bone-chilling coolness. A perfect set for a horror film.

"Yeah?" a voice echoed up from the basement.

"I'm here about a bed for the night." I called out to the bodiless male voice.

"Oh. I'll be up in a second. Just doing the laundry."

A few minutes later a man appeared with a young girl in tow. She had attached herself to his side like a limpet and was staring wide-eyed at the stranger standing in their entrance hall.

"A bed for tonight. Won't have any trouble there. You can have a whole floor to yourself if you want it," he laughed and led me into a small office. "Here you go. Room 10."

The little girl perched herself on the desk, silently examining me.

"Great. I see you're not very busy," I said, picking up my bags.

He shook his head, not seeming to be particularly worried by this state of affairs. "No, too early in the season. And the weather's terrible right now."

"Yes, I know. I'm only going to be here for the one night. I'll be catching the bus out tomorrow morning."

The young man paused as he was closing up his ledger book and looked up at me in surprise. "Bus out in the morning?"

"Yes, that's right. There must be some bus that goes through here tomorrow."

"No, there's no bus service on Sunday. The next bus will be on Monday afternoon. And that doesn't even stop in Waterville. You'd have to hitch five miles back up the road."

I dropped my bags onto the floor with a thunk of horror. I had to be in Cork by Monday morning. I had a car rental set up and an interview with Ireland's premier restauranteur, Myrtle Allen. I couldn't miss that.

"How am I going to get out of here? I have to be in Cork by Monday." My voice rose in desperation.

The girl wriggled excitedly on the desk. This stranger was providing more entertainment than she had expected.

"You could always hitch?"

"You don't sound too confident."

"Well, traffic's pretty slow through here right now. And with the rain, I don't know what your chances are of getting a lift right round the Ring." He shrugged his shoulders and shook his head sadly.

"Is there anywhere around here that I can rent a car? I just have to make it to Killarney, and then I can catch a train from there."

"Rent a car? Here?" he laughed, and then seeing my worried expression, hiccuped to a stop. "Wait, there might be something." He rummaged in a desk drawer and brought out a tattered business card. "I think one of the tour buses will be coming through here tomorrow. Give them a call and see if they can book you a seat. You'll have to sit through a tour, but at least it'll get you out of the Ring."

I grabbed the telephone number with relief and dashed out to the hall pay-phone. The number rang for a few moments and then a broad Irish voice spoke on the other end of the line.

"Deros Tours."

I explained my predicament as clearly as I could. There was a few moments silence on the other end of the line.

"You want to pick up our Ring of Kerry bus tour in Waterville?" the woman's voice asked.

"That's right."

"But that's half-way through the tour."

"I know. I just want to get a guaranteed lift into Killarney."

She seemed unconvinced. "But it'll take you four hours on the tour bus. And you'll have to pay full fare regardless."

I assured her that an all-day excursion at full rate was, at this point, a dream come true. She grudgingly agreed to allow me on the bus and told me to be in the centre of Waterville at noon the next day to flag it down. "It'll have Deros Tours across the front. He'll be expecting you." And with typical Irish bluntness, she added: "And don't go and catch a lift with someone else now. We'll be holding that seat open for you on your word."

And with that guilt-inducing remark, she hung up.

I found out later that evening, as I prowled the echoing corridors of the hostel, that I was not its sole occupant. A trio of Irish girls had also escaped from the persistent rain to spend the night in the hostel. The three - Anne, Sheila and Mary - were on a weekend hitching trip from Limerick. With bad weather and limited tourists, they had run into the same transportation problems as I had.

"Sneem," Anne said with a sigh, her hand enveloping the hot mug of tea I had poured out for her.

The other two nodded their heads in sad agreement.

"What's a sneem?" I asked.

"Not what. Where. It's a tourist town about half an hour's drive from here. We got a lift as far as Sneem, and that was it."

"We couldn't get out," Sheila put in. "We must have waited three hours in the rain before we started to walk. We got out of Sneem, thinking we'd have a better chance of getting a ride, but all we could get were offers of rides back into Sneem."

"Kind of like the Bermuda Triangle of villages, hmmm?" I added.

There was silent agreement from all three.

They had finally managed to get a lift back to Waterville, which only put them further away from Killarney. They had to return home by Sunday night in order to make their college exams on Monday. I told them about my chat with Deros Tours.

"Do you think they could fit us on?" Mary asked hopefully.

"I don't know. She said they'd hold one seat. But if they're not full, I don't see why they wouldn't take you as well. It'll cost you six pounds though."

"Six pounds!" A snort of disgust from Sheila. "That's disgusting. It's only a two hour ride from here to Killarney."

I smiled. "Not the way they drive it, it isn't."

The next day dawned sunny. We gathered after breakfast on the gravel drive in front of Waterville Heights, as I had come to think of the Gothic monstrosity, each of us looking hesitantly skyward.

"Well, it's not raining," I offered, as we started into the centre of the village.

"Not yet," Sheila added.

A few tentative tourists had made their way out to the beach promenade and were walking along as the Atlantic angrily smashed the beach. At the end of the road, a bright pink mansion could be seen resting against the sand. It was cordoned off with fencing and a variety of Keep Off signs.

"Is that Charlie Chaplin's home?" I asked.

Sheila followed my gaze down to the waterfront. "I don't know." She pointed past the pink house to another large estate. "I do know that that's the new Club Med."

"Club Med?" I was astonished. I couldn't believe that such a sleepy, rainswept place could be home to grinning *gentil organisateurs* and tropical cocktails. "You've got to be kidding."

"No. They're just getting it fixed up now."

"Maybe then they'll have bus service," grumbled Mary.

To our surprise, a tiny village shop was open on a Sunday morning. We stocked up on the only cheap, transportable food available in Ireland, namely potato chips and pop, and sat down on the curb to wait for the bus.

It didn't take long.

"Here comes one," Anne shouted as a tour bus rounded the bend and came trundling slowly along the narrow road. She jumped up and began to wave frantically.

The bus did not slow down, probably because it said Patrick's Tours across the near side. The tourists and the bus driver slowly motored along the beach watching Anne hop around the sidewalk frantically.

"Maybe the next one," Sheila comforted Anne as she weakly settled down to rest on the curb.

Before long another silver tour bus rounded the bend. I was determined that this time things would be done with a bit more subtlety. I looked for a name on the bus, but there was none. I waved my hand in a flagging motion, rather like a cross between the queen's wave and a military salute. The bus driver slowed down a bit, looked at me, and then started to pick up speed.

To hell with subtlety. I ran out into the road, manically waving my hands in the air. The bus screeched to a stop.

The bus driver, an older man, slid open a window and stared down at me in concern. "What is it? An accident or something?"

"No. Are you the Deros Tour bus?"

His concern turned to laughter. "No, I'm Denny's Tours. Deros is right behind us. Give them another five minutes, Dear. And stop running in front of moving vehicles, or there really will be an accident."

With that, he slammed his window closed and continued up the road.

Sure enough, the Deros Tour bus arrived five minutes later, its name painted clearly along its side. It eased to a stop in front of us, and the door opened with a hiss. The bus driver stepped off and examined the group of us on the sidewalk.

"Who is Kim Herdman?" he asked.

"I am." I stood up and picked up my bags. He handed me my filled-out ticket form and took the six pounds. "I was wondering if you might have some extra seats. These three girls are trying to get to Killarney as well."

"Three seats, hmmm. You get on the bus and I'll have a wee chat with these young ladies."

The bus was stiflingly warm and filled with American tourists. I had met a few "Ugly Americans" so far on this trip, but more often than not I had found Americans to be pleasant travelling companions. These, however, were a different breed of tourists: well fed, middle-aged, their arms overloaded with camcorders and Samsonite carryalls. A world away from the travellers I had been meeting.

I settled myself in the back row of the bus beside a teenaged boy who was determinedly trying to block out the rest of the world. His eyes were shut and the earphones of his Walkman were embedded deeply in either side of his head. I could detect nothing except a thumping bass.

Five minutes later, the three girls trooped onto the bus behind the driver. He placed Sheila beside a lady further up in the bus, and seated Anne and Mary beside me in the back row.

"We got on!" Anne whispered to Mary as they settled themselves in their seats. "And we only had to pay four pounds!"

"Four pounds?" I questioned.

"Yes," Mary beamed. "We said we didn't have any more than that. So he let us on anyway. Wasn't that nice?"

I nodded my head, wondering whether that extra few pounds would ever find its way back to Deros Tours or go directly into the pocket of the nearest publican.

With a clanging of gears, the bus lurched forward and the driver began the tepidly humourous patter that was to continue for the next four hours. "And this is beautiful Waterville, known to people all over the world ..."

I tuned him out and turned to Anne and Mary who were chattering to an elderly American gentleman.

"And which part of Ireland are you from?" he asked me.

I fought back the desire to imitate a broad Irish accent and instead said, "Vancouver. Canada."

"Oh. I'm from Florida. Sarasota."

A hefty young man seated in front of us swiveled around. "Did you say Sarasota? My folks live there now. They love it." His accent was midwestern and had that loud, invasive tone that cuts across European museums between June and August. His wife was pretty in a trashy kind of way, with bright red lipstick and sticky candy-floss eyelashes.

"I'm from Ohio. We are, I mean. Me and Nancy. We're on our honeymoon."

The Floridian was not pleased at having his conversation interrupted by this loud individual and turned his attention to the window. Anne and Mary stared at the quarterback from Ohio as if he had come from another planet. I jumped in to fill the silence.

"Are you enjoying the trip?"

He took a large handful of potato chips and then gestured the bag at us. "It's okay. You know, it's green and everything, but the weather is shitty. It's better than this back home."

"We'd be wearing shorts now, you know, at home," Nancy contributed.

"Yeah, and the food is horrible. All they've got are these." He held up the plastic bag of potato chips. "I feel like I've been living on chips for the past week. And they don't even call them chips. What do they call them here?"

"Crisps," Mary volunteered.

"Crisps. Is that all these people eat? Potatoes? Is it like their only crop or something? God, you'd think they'd find something else to eat."

The irony of his statement was not lost on Anne. "They've kept us from going hungry," she said softly, an undertone of anger in her voice.

Such subtlety, however, was lost on our American friend. He turned back in his seat and continued to complain to his new bride.

I turned my attention back to the scenery. The bus was now winding its way away from the beach, leaving the nice weather of Waterville behind. One minute we were in sunshine, the next we were engulfed in a thick, impenetrable cloud.

"I'm sorry, but there's nothing we can do about this mist," the bus driver offered apologetically. "We have a saying in Ireland. If you don't like the weather, just wait fifteen minutes and it'll change." Dutiful laughter bubbled up from the passengers. "Well, folks, this is a real shame. If we didn't have this horrible mist here, you would be looking at some of the most beautiful scenery in Ireland. On the left there would be some typical examples of local architecture."

All heads swiveled to the left. You couldn't see a thing. We were totally covered in a mist as thick and milky as clam chowder.

"And on the right now you would see some of the highest cliffs in the Ring of Kerry."

There was a jerk as necks swiveled to the right. Everyone stared out the windows with an air of simulated interest. It was like a tour of "Ireland for the blind".

"Yes, it's a dramatic twelve-hundred-foot drop to the frothing Atlantic below."

I heard the whirr of a camcorder and turned to see a man filming through the window. I don't know what he thought he was filming, but it certainly wasn't the frothing Atlantic below him. I closed my eyes and settled down into the warmth of my seat for a short nap. There wasn't anything to see and I could live without this aural soundtrack to the Ring of Kerry.

"My God, it's Sneem."

I awoke to find the fog gone and the bus chugging its way over a bridge into a tiny village. Mary and Anne were in stitches.

"What is it?"

"It's SNEEM! We can't escape it." Anne giggled out.

"It's your destiny," I muttered and closed my eyes once again.

But it seemed we were all destined to visit Sneem, if only to enrich the pockets of the tourist shops on the main street. The bus pulled to a stop in front of a row of woollen shops, and the driver announced we were going to have a short break.

He mispronounced short. He meant shopping.

Half an hour later, we took off again, a satisfied if heavier crowd, laden with bags of Irish woollens. We headed inland, this time towards the Black Valley. The dramatic emerald mountains and gorges were eerily beautiful against the slate grey clouds and shivers of mist. Their silent desolation, however, would have impressed me more if I could have appreciated it in silence. I was forced instead to listen to the bus driver's cute, history-by-numbers talk.

"And for people living in the Black Valley, well, it's a difficult life. The modern world has never truly entered their homes. Their only transportation is on the back of a donkey. They must butcher their own meat and make their own bread," he nattered on.

"And when things are really bad, they eat small animals that are killed on the road," Anne added sarcastically. "What is that man talking about? He's going to make all these people think we're backward. We're not peasants!"

"Do you think they believe it?" Mary asked me.

I glanced at the people around us; they appeared to be lapping up every word. "I'm afraid so."

My seatmate, the fifteen-year-old with premature deafness, had said nothing in the three hours we had been on the road. I opened up a bag of chips and offered it to him. He took a handful and looked up at me, as if checking to see whether I was cool enough to communicate with. I obviously must have measured up, for he pulled out his earphones with a pop.

"Thanks," he said.

"Don't worry about it. Are you enjoying the tour?"

He raised his eyebrows until they met the shaggy bottoms of his bangs. "This is my second tour so far this week." I thought he had finished, but he was only summoning up enough energy to continue. "I hate this stuff."

I nodded my head and attempted to remember the boredom of adolescence. "Where are you from?"

"Chicago."

"You're with your parents?"

"Yeah." he said, with a furtive nod up the aisle of the bus. "I like it back here though."

"So you can listen to your music?"

"Yeah, and pretend I'm at home." With another nod of thanks for the nourishment, he replaced the earphones and drifted off again.

It seemed hard to believe, but we were almost at Killarney. What I could have driven in an hour had taken me most of the day to traverse. One more stop and I'd be back in civilization.

The bus eased to a stop beside a scenic lake. As this was a photo stop, everyone rushed to the lakeside for some snaps. The three girls and myself, being non-snapping types, were prevailed upon to perform the duties for everyone else.

After four hours of loud, simplistic comments about Ireland's rich history, I wanted nothing more to do with anyone on that bus. And yet, as they queued up for me to snap their pictures, arms entwined, teeth showing, they stopped looking like insensitive tourists. They became people. People with families and friends, with dogs and slide projectors. People who became gawkily shy and embarrassingly human as they waited for me to say "Fromage".

My seatmate, reunited briefly with his parents, managed a momentary lifting of his upper lip. Nancy and her oafish husband seemed almost charming as they stood cuddling on the lakefront. Almost. Even Anne, Mary and Sheila, whose opinion of Americans had soured over the past four hours, were smiling as they took the photos. Perhaps everyone can identify with wanting a snapshot of a happy memory.

With the photos finished, we clambered back on the bus for the short, remaining trip to Killarney.

"It's almost over," I whispered to Anne, who had only just managed to control her temper throughout the afternoon.

The bus driver's voice boomed over the speakers. "And here, ladies and gentleman, is the sight you've been waiting for. Does everyone have their cameras ready? It's coming up on the right side of the road. There it is, Ireland's own leprechaun crossing!" We leaned out the window to see a small placard sign with a leprechaun on it. Anne groaned as the bus driver droned on. "And there he is, ladies and gentleman! Did everyone get a picture? You had to really be fast. It's not often you spot one of them!"

The three of us couldn't hold it in any longer. While cameras snapped around us, we broke into laughter so loud that it dragged my musical seatmate from his contemplations.

"Hey, what's going on?" he asked, turning down his volume.

"Nothing. Nothing at all. You just missed the best part of Ireland, that's all," I laughed out.

"Oh, that's okay then," he said and, putting his earphones back in, leaned back and closed his eyes once again.

x *cuisine, irish style*

Carroway's Car Rentals stood in an old part of Cork near the river. The small streetfront office looked as if it had survived intact from the twenties, with its dark wood and mouldering furniture. From the amount of dust on the shelves and the stacks of loose papers everywhere, it looked like it had last been cleaned about that time, too.

"Good morning," a tall, thin man in a jaunty tweed cap called out to the four of us as we stood hesitantly on the doorstep. "Come on in if you're coming."

I wasn't alone in my silent contemplations of the rental office. Nat and Van, my two Australian friends, whom I'd met as arranged in Cork, and Tom, the Canadian I'd met in Skye and Dublin, who we'd found by surprise at the hostel, were with me.

We stepped into the small office, filling what little extra space there was.

"I'm Kim Herdman. I called you a few days ago to make a reservation for a car?"

The car rental man took a cigarette from his mouth and dangled it above a stack of papers. Grey ash dropped onto the top sheet.

"A car reservation. Let me see. What was the name again?"

"Herdman, Kim Herdman."

He leafed through the pile, scattering ash over the desk, before producing a piece of paper. The tweed cap looked like it was about to slip off his greasy hair.

"Here it is. Kim Herdman. Called on the fifteenth. Would you like to have a seat?" He gestured with his cigarette towards the only seat in the room. "Just have to ask you a few questions for the insurance."

I handed him my international driver's license. He rummaged underneath a waxy parcel before pulling out a long form and replacing his cigarette with a pen.

"This is about all the information I need," he said, glancing at the license and scribbling away, "except for your profession."

"Journalist," I answered absent-mindedly. I was trying to read the date on an ancient copy of National Geographic sitting on a side table. It said 1968.

"Did you say journalist?" The car rental man had stopped writing, his narrow face slackening in dismay.

"Yes, that's right. Journalist."

"I'm afraid we cannot insure journalists on our vehicles."

The four of us looked over in surprise.

"What do you mean, you cannot insure journalists?" I asked.

He raised his hands in a gesture of universal servitude, enslaved as he was to a higher master. "It's the policy of the insurance company." He paused then as an idea struck. "Do you by any chance have another profession?"

"Another profession? Isn't one enough?"

His hangdog grimace lifted in a rakish grin that revealed a blackened tooth. "Not if you're a journalist and you want to rent a car."

"Well, I am a journalist and I want to rent a car. Why can't I be insured?" I asked angrily.

"Too big a risk."

"Too big a risk? Who else won't they insure?"

"Military officials, football athletes, dog racing aficionados," he listed them off in a matter-of-fact fashion.

"Dog racing aficionados?" I repeated incredulously.

The man shook his head sadly. "Yes, terrible accident rates, I'm afraid."

"Well, then, what about a writer? I'm a writer as well."

He checked the list. "No, I'm afraid they won't insure writers either."

"Drink too much, I suppose?"

The man shook his head in sorrowful agreement. "Yes, and you know what that can do to a person's driving abilities."

I was beginning to lose my patience. "Look, I have an appointment in Shengarry in a few hours. I need a car. Can't you just write down something?"

The man sat back in his creaking wooden chair, the kind that pivots on an ancient spring, and picked up his cigarette. He puffed meditatively for a few moments. "Do you not have any other profession I could write down?"

I paused to run over my resume. A caterer? I have made the occasional tray of canapés. Or therapist? Counselling a depressed friend must count for some kind of career training.

"Poet? I'm a poet, or at least that's what my editor says. Is that insurable?"

He snapped forward in his seat and ran his thumb down the list. "Yes, they are!"

"Yahoo!" Nat called out in mock excitement. "We're going as poets!"

He filled in the final line on the sheet and pushed it across the desk for me to sign.

I didn't bother to ask why poets were thought to be a better risk than writers, especially as they seemed to me far more likely to do romantically dangerous things to themselves. I grabbed the car keys and was out of the office in a flash. Tom, Nat and Van scurried out after me.

"You do know how to drive in Ireland, don't you?" The car rental man called out nervously after us. He was standing on the front step, bouncing up and down on the balls of his feet.

"Yes, I know," I answered in exasperation. "Drive on the left."

I unlocked the car door and hurriedly climbed in. I was preparing to reach across to unlock the other door when I heard a tapping on the window. Nat was gesturing to me from outside.

"What is it, Nat?" I rolled down the window. "I want to get out of here while we've still got the chance."

She pointed at the bare dash in front of me and then at the steering wheel on the other side. "You're on the passenger side, Kim."

I avoided the eye of the car rental man as I got out of the car and walked quickly around to the driver's side.

The first mile was the most difficult. I had never driven on the "wrong" side of the road before, and couldn't get over the feeling that at any moment a vehicle was going to come barrelling down the road at me head on.

"How am I doing?" I asked as we zoomed down the highway out of Cork.

"You're doing fine, Kim," Nat said with wary enthusiasm.

"Thanks for the overwhelming vote of support. Am I doing that badly?" I turned to look at Nat, unthinkingly turning the steering wheel in the same direction. We swerved towards a small car packed with schoolkids. Nat grabbed the wheel and steered us back into my lane.

"Keep your eyes on the road, Kim! Concentrate on what you're doing!"

Sulkily, I turned my concentration back to the highway.

"You're doing fine, Kim," Van offered from the back seat.

"Yeah, Kim. Just relax," was Tom's back seat contribution.

Relax! They wanted me to relax! With cars shooting on and off the highway in every direction, most of them seeming to defy every road regulation I had ever known? I wasn't going to be able to relax until I had parked this thing in the lot of some cosy-looking pub and had a pint in my hand.

"Now, it's not that far before we reach our roundabout," Nat said soothingly as we left the outskirts of Cork behind us.

"Roundabout? What's a roundabout?" I asked, thinking of Yes songs and swirling guitar solos. I didn't want to experience any roundabout. I was just getting used to this highway.

"It's a circular exit."

"A circular what?"

"Everyone drives into the roundabout and you just circle around until you reach your exit and then you shoot off."

"Like Piccadilly Circus?" I had visions of being caught up in a merry-go-round of automobiles, lit by neon signs and populated with hippies.

"Exactly. Don't you have roundabouts in Canada?" Van leaned forward in her seat to chat convivially in my ear.

"No, or at least I don't think we do. Do we, Tom?"

Tom agreed that Canadians were too advanced for such rustic highway exits.

"Here's our sign," Nat pointed out. "The roundabout is in 500 metres."

I gripped the steering wheel tightly between my fingers. Signs were now flashing before us with greater rapidity.

Roundabout 250 metres.

100 metres.

Suddenly we were in the middle of an asphalt circle and Nat was shouting for me to circle to the left. Around I whizzed like some crazed mouse in a pavement covered wheel. There was a momentary vision of another car and somewhat worried-looking driver before I saw the sign for Shengarry and then the opening, and shot out of the round-about like a cork from a champagne bottle. We had advanced along the secondary road for about one hundred metres before I released my death grip on the steering wheel.

"Very good, Kim," Nat laughed, releasing some of her own tension. "I knew you could do it."

Light applause arose from the back seat.

We drove into a small village, the main street busy with women doing their morning shopping. I relaxed my shoulders a little and sank back into the driver's seat.

"This really isn't that bad," I said and turned to smile at Tom and Van. "I think I've got the hang of this now."

"Kim! Watch out!"

I slammed on the brakes and we screeched to a stop in the middle of the road. The four of us turned around to see a middle-aged woman gasping beside the open door of her car. I had missed it by a matter of inches. She dazedly looked at me as I made a bashful apology through the window and then started up the road again.

"Kim," Van started out tentatively, "would you like one of us to drive for a bit?"

I dropped the trio in a small fishing town called Youghal. It looked like an interesting stopover for the afternoon. I then headed back inland to the village of Shengarry, and from there took a country road no wider than a single car's width until I reached the gates of Ballymaloe House, one of Ireland's better known country house hotels.

The wooden gate was open, and I steered my car onto the drive. It wound for a mile or so through rolling meadows dotted with sheep and wildflowers. As I drew nearer the house, I could see men putting golf balls on a neatly cropped field.

The drive curled to its end before a two-storey stone house, the front of which was almost obscured by a thick covering of ivy. The lawn was dotted with white wrought-iron benches where several women sat reading in the sun. I parked the car and wandered past them to the front door.

I approached a young woman sitting in the front hall and asked for Myrtle Allen. She pointed me outside, and said that Myrtle would join me in a few moments. I wandered out to take shade under a patterned sun umbrella, glad of the cotton blouse and loose skirt I had chosen to wear.

A few minutes later, I felt a hand on my shoulder and turned to see Myrtle Allen standing behind me.

"Hello," Her voice was pleasant but firm, her stare direct but not threatening. "I'm so sorry to have kept you waiting. Would you like a cup of tea?" She settled herself in a seat opposite mine and gestured to a young woman to bring us tea.

She must have been in her early sixties, with the grey hair and simple skirt and blouse of a grandmother. And yet her manner was more that of a forty-year-old, with a confident curiosity and youthful energy. We chatted about my travels and interviews in Ireland until the tea arrived.

"How did you get started in the restaurant business?" I asked as I sipped from a dainty china teacup. "Did you have any training in the field?"

She laughed and took a sip from her own cup. "No, I was just the wife of a farmer. I really started all of this as a hobby."

I smiled as a Jaguar pulled into the drive, piloted, I was sure, by some wealthy captain of industry. "Was it quite a surprise then, to suddenly become the flagbearer of 'authentic' Irish cuisine?"

"Yes," she mused, "I suppose it was. I just always did what I wanted. I cooked what I wanted to cook, and it happened that I wanted to cook our own food." She gestured to the rolling countryside around us, and the hens pecking idly along the drive. "We grow our own fruit, have our own hens and at one time even butchered our own meat. It was just the way we lived."

"Your particular style of cooking, where did that come from?"

"I grew up in an Anglo-Irish tradition, where you find a number of different influences on the cooking, from English to traditional Irish to Continental. All of these blended together into a single cuisine, which people now call Irish Country House cooking. It was just the kind of foods I ate when I was a child."

After three years of operation, a favourable review had shot her and her restaurant into culinary orbit and made a star of a working mother recreating the simple foods she had grown up with. And this was in the sixties, decades before traditional cuisine came into vogue.

I mentioned that she had taken a leap into the unknown with her restaurant, especially as every other cook at the time was attempting to recreate the latest Parisian dish.

Myrtle laughed her warm, rousing laugh, and I was struck by its unpretentious sound. "Yes, I would have been serving poached rhubarb when everyone else was breaking their neck trying to get kiwi fruit."

Not satisfied with being a success on her home turf, Allen had turned her attention to foreign ground and opened the Irish Restaurant in Paris. She went on to write many cookbooks and open the hotel at Ballymaloe House. She was now gladly shifting some of the workload onto her children.

"What are you going to do for your retirement years?" I asked as I drained my teacup.

She smiled and looked over at the house. "Run Ballymaloe, I suppose, and watch my grandchildren grow up."

It sounded like a pleasant enough retirement to me.

As noon arrived in tandem with the end of our interview, Myrtle was kind enough to invite me to stay for lunch. She left me in the capable hands of a young waitress, as she had a wedding party that evening to look after. As the waitress seated me at one of the small tables that dotted the blue and white dining room, I glanced nervously at the other diners, most of whom were older and decidedly more prosperous than me.

"Start on the outside and work your way in," I murmured to myself as I examined the variety of eating utensils on the table.

I looked up to see a trio of middle-aged women at a nearby table gazing at my legs. I followed their gaze. I was not wearing stockings, and I'm afraid weeks of walking had made my abused feet and legs look a little the worse for wear. I tucked them underneath the linen tablecloth and shot the women a brazenly direct smile. They smiled weakly in return and turned their attention back to their own table.

The lunch was a buffet and, as if from some unseen signal, the other patrons rose in a single body and headed towards a heavily laden table. I followed behind, my nose tickling with the luscious smell of roast meats and grilled vegetables.

The long table was topped with a variety of foods, starting with tossed salads and a cool whipped fish mousse. Plaice and roast pork glistened beside a scented leg of roast lamb, its centre dripping small beads of pink juice. Ratatouille, pastry encrusted pepper tarts, baby potatoes glistening in butter and tossed with parsley - the table was filled. I loaded my plate with as much food as I felt I could decently carry back to my table, and then settled back to enjoy.

It was, as Myrtle Allen had stated, simple food. There were no strong seasonings or fancy sauces, but the quality of the food and the subtlety of the cooking shone through.

I was not the only one who was enjoying my lunch. The trio of ladies headed back for seconds before I had even finished my first helping. Dessert arrived on a trolley, and I hesitated before tasting anything. Two months of thrifty eating had reduced my appetite to desiring little more than a soup and salad for lunch. The meal I had just eaten could have kept me going for a week.

"Oh, come now, Miss. Do try one," my waitress encouraged me.

"Could I just have a little taste of several?" I asked.

"Certainly." She picked up a dessert plate and topped it with fresh gooseberry fool, a small slice of raspberry charlotte, and some cullageen, which is a seaweed custard scented with vanilla.

I nibbled at the various tastes and textures, one eye on the women at the neighbouring table. For all their poshness, they weren't shy about their appetites. The one who had gazed with the most disgust at my lack of legwear insisted on two plates of dessert, and I think would have gone for a third if the waitress had not pushed on to the next table.

The freshly brewed pot of tea was a lovely end to a perfect meal. I sipped slowly and sat back in the chair, feeling my stomach expand to an amazing rotundity.

As I stood in the scented washroom after lunch, drying my hands on a thick, plush towel, I thought of the spartan life I had been living. A thick slab of lavender soap, rich with scented oil? I hadn't seen that in weeks. And towels, lush, sumptuous ones you can bury your face into and never feel that horrid cottony rasp? I'd forgotten how heavenly this all felt. It was going to be difficult returning to hostel life after luxury like this.

Tom, Nat, and Van were waiting for me in a teashop in the centre of Youghal. We shared a pot of tea as I regaled them with the sensual details of luncheon at Ballymaloe House. As the afternoon drifted to a close they teased me about my hamfisted driving and we reminisced about the times Nat, Van and I had spent together in Glasgow and Dingle. The afternoon sun had just begun to sink towards the Irish Sea as we made our way out of the teashop and back onto the road for Cork.

Sighting a scenic overlook, I pulled off quickly to the side of the road. An emerald bluff dipped down from the highway to a valley of patchwork fields before plummeting into the sea. It was like something from an Irish Tourist Board ad. A perfect postcard photo op.

It would be the last time I'd see Nat and Van on this trip. They were staying on in the United Kingdom to work for six months, while Tom and I moved on to the continent. I had already planned to meet him again in Paris in six days.

The warm summer breeze brushed my skirt against my bare legs as the three of us hugged each other on that beautiful headland. I could hear in the background Tom snapping photos of us as I looked over my two friends' shoulders to the sea. That's where I was headed. East. The Continent.

A new adventure.

The Continent

xi Paris: city of love

Sun filled the cabin of the DC 10 as we broke through the heavy armour of grey clouds over Dublin and banked towards Paris. For the past two months, I had experienced some of the worst weather Britain and Ireland had seen in years. Rain, hail, sleet, even snow had greeted me. Sniffling colds and perpetually damp shoes had been my constant companions. But now, finally, I was headed for the glorious warmth of the Continent.

An hour later the plane circled low over sleeping Paris. Wide-eyed, I stared down at the City of Love. Lit by the thousands of white sparkling lights lining the spoked streets, it reminded me of a fairground at night. The Eiffel Tower, floodlit in the centre of the city, looked like some delicate confection stuck on the top of a cake.

At Orly, I was hustled through the EEC passport lineup - it was too late for either me or the customs officer to care where I came from - and found myself on a bus headed into the city. The magical glow of my arrival, however, faded with each highway sign we passed.

I couldn't read any of them.

We hissed to a stop on a silent Parisian street and with a sense of panic I realized the bus driver was pointing at me.

"*Ici*?" I asked plaintively.

"*Oui, oui, mademoiselle. Ici, pour vous*."

I glanced around at the faces staring up at me. What must they be thinking? That I'm so stupid I didn't realize that I would be arriving in a strange city where they speak a language I have not uttered in fifteen years?

I took a deep breath and stepped off the bus. Grey stone buildings stretched along the street, the occasional red awning of a closed cafe dotting the sidewalk. I could have been anywhere from the Left Bank to the *Arc de Triomphe*.

The bus pulled away in a cloud of diesel fumes while I cursed my stupidity for not having taken a taxi from the airport. Two other women had got off the bus and were walking towards a large, lit building. I raised my hand in a plea for help.

"*Excusez-moi. Parlez-vous anglais*?"

They turned at the sound of my voice and the fair-haired one smiled warmly. Both were in their late teens and carried backpacks.

"Yes, I speak English. Do you need some help?" she said with what I recognized as an English accent.

"Do I! I'm trying to find the youth hostel. The bus driver dropped me here with you, and I'm afraid I have no idea where I am."

The English girl translated what I had said for the other woman, who nodded her head in sympathy before answering in a rapid patter of French.

"Yes, Ann-Marie says that you're quite a distance from the hostel. The bus driver dropped you here thinking you would take the Metro to the hostel." The Englishwoman gestured with her thumb to the building behind us. "But I don't think you should take the Metro by yourself, not at this time of night." She had another brief conversation with the other woman. "No, it's too confusing and dangerous for you to travel now. Ann-Marie will get a taxi for you."

As good as her word, Ann-Marie trotted down the street in search of a taxi, leaving the two of us standing silently together.

"My name is Kim," I offered.

"Julia."

"Are you returning home from a trip?" I continued, hoping for some conversation to fill the silence.

Julia absently readjusted the buckles on her rucksack. "Sort of. We're just spending a few weeks with friends in Paris before heading home. Ann Marie and I actually live in a small village an hour and a half outside of Paris."

"Really? What's its name? Perhaps I've heard of it."

"Oh, I don't think so." She shook her head and smiled. "It's very small."

"Come on," I urged, "What is it?"

Julia sighed with good-humoured resignation. "Trosly."

I could not have been more staggered if she had physically knocked the wind out of me. "Trosly?" I stuttered out. "Do you mean Trosly-Breuil?"

Julia stopped examining her knapsack and looked up at my face. "Yes, that's right. I work for a small religious community up there ..."

"L'Arche?" I cut in.

Now it was her turn to look surprised. "You've heard of it?"

"Yes, I have. I'm just stopping in Paris for a few days to do some work and then I'm going there. I'm a journalist. I'm going to interview Jean Vanier, the man who started up L'Arche."

"You're here to speak with Jean?"

I couldn't believe it. Of all the people I should turn to for help on a Paris street corner in the middle of the night, how incredible that it should be two citizens of a religious community I was making a special trip to visit, a place which boasts a population of only a few hundred!

We were still giggling over this when a sleek black Citroen taxi pulled up in front of us. Ann-Marie came running down the street after it. I threw my bags inside and offered fervent and grateful thanks to my heaven-sent benefactors. As the taxi slid soundlessly away along the empty streets, I could still see them waving goodbye from the Metro station.

Who says miracles never happen?

Having had only one night reserved at the hostel, I was thrust out onto the streets to hunt for further lodging the next morning. The Paris that had struck me as so intimidating the previous night was now a gracious grey stone world lit by warm sunlight. I wandered the streets in an orgiastic haze, overwhelmed by the city's architectural splendour. Certainly London and Bath had some beautiful exteriors, but they were nothing like the avenues of Paris! Every tree-lined street, no matter how small, seemed to exhibit a gust of *joie de vivre* that was as palpable as the rich buttery smell of croissants emanating from the nearest *patisseries.*

But there was still the language problem. I decided to try out my shaky French at my first stop of the morning, the *boulangerie.*

"*Bonjour,*" I said in my best French accent as I sidled up to the counter of the yeasty smelling bakery.

An older woman and her young assistant looked up from behind an assortment of thick sandwiches. These slabs of french bread were sliced in half and then filled with cheeses and meats, lettuce and tomatoes, looking, with their haphazard bounty, unlike any geometrically exact sandwich you might get in North America.

"*Bonjour,*" the baker answered and then hesitated, waiting for me to order.

I looked from her to the shelves and then back up once again, my throat dry. "*Excusez moi, je suis arrivé à Paris hier. Mon français n'est pas bon,*" I said and paused, hoping for some sympathy to ease me over the linguistic bumps ahead.

"*Non, non,*" the older woman tutted. "*Vous parlez français très bien.*"

Her assistant nodded her head in smiling approval and an elderly matron who had been searching for the perfect loaf joined us at the counter, gesturing with her knobbly hand for me to continue my efforts at their language.

"*Je veux,*" I started out and then paused to look at the rows of sandwiches. What the hell was the French word for sandwich? I pointed at a luscious looking baguette crammed with cheese and lettuce, but the baker shook her head and laughingly waggled a finger in my face.

"*Non, vous parlez pour moi.*"

Sandwich, sandwich. What could I say to describe a sandwich?

"*Je veux le pain ici.*" I pointed to the sandwich again.

"*Avec la salade?*" the baker asked, motioning towards a sandwich filled with lettuce and tomato in addition to the cheese.

"*Oui. Merci.*"

The elderly matron clapped her hands at my effort while the young assistant retrieved my baguette and placed it on the top of the counter. I paid the sum while the woman and the baker chattered away in French, no doubt critiquing my performance.

"*Au revoir,*" I called out in farewell, munching on my baguette and filled with the courage to attempt a more difficult linguistic target.

"*Au revoir,*" the three answered in unison.

I munched my way towards the American Express office near the Opéra to retrieve a note from Tom. It listed his address while in Paris as a hotel in the Ledru Rollin district.

I spotted him as soon as I entered the hotel foyer. He was sipping at a soup-bowl sized cup of coffee, his lips tilted at a teasing angle. His eyes met mine over the mass of sweaty kids in tattered shorts and t-shirts, and I felt my heart lift. Nothing like a familiar face in a strange city to brighten your morning, I told myself as I went forward to give him a friendly hug in greeting.

"You got my note," he said in my ear as I felt his unshaven cheek brush against my own.

"Uhm hmm. Went there first thing this morning."

He took another sip from his coffee. "So you haven't seen Paris yet?"

"Not much more than the trip here on the metro."

"Ah then, mademoiselle," he flopped over in a courtly bow which was made difficult by his full cup of coffee, "Paris awaits!"

I booked myself a room for that evening, and, taking his arm, started off on our day's outing.

I had always imagined Paris as warm and spring-like, rather like the Doris Day song. In my imagination, I could feel a warm breeze tickling the chestnut blossoms while I danced along the Left Bank with Fred Astaire. Paris as seen by Paramount. But this July day was hot and humid, with temperatures in the high eighties by mid-morning. My sweaters and pants were relegated to the bottom of my bag, cold and rainy Ireland long forgotten.

Tom and I spent the day happily wandering the streets of Paris, a sunlit world rich with sensual decadence and classical formality. We ate and browsed and laughed and shopped. We sat in a sidewalk cafe and sipped iced coffee while Parisians listlessly sauntered by as if bored with their own sophistication, and finished the day with a dinner in a romantic restaurant in the Latin Quarter. It was a lovely introduction to Paris.

My interview the next morning at the Jeu de Paume Art Gallery scored another coup for my improving linguistic skills. It was conducted almost completely in French, and gave me both a good overview of the gallery's collection of modern art and an interesting column.

My next attempt at communicating *à français* was with a young French Canadian couple who were staying at my hotel. I was asked to translate a question for them from a young Texan, and soon discovered that they were not French but *Québécois*. I had read about the latest separation crisis in Quebec and was anxious for news from home.

"The referendum will be held fairly soon, I believe," the young man answered my question in French with perfect English. His girlfriend, however, spoke no English at all.

"Well, what's the mood? Do you think Quebec is going to vote to separate?"

The young man seemed embarrassed by my directness. "Perhaps. Feelings are running pretty high there now. I think a lot of people feel that we'd be better off on our own. But maybe," he offered diplomatically, "tempers will cool down."

I leaned forward, speaking in a mixture of French and English. "But you know that English Canada doesn't want you to go?"

He leaned away from me, his embarrassment turning to weary cynicism. "I'm sure that *you* don't want us to go."

"No, it's not just me. Other than a few crackpots out there who've nothing better to do than stamp on the flag, people want Canada to stay together."

It was ironic that our conversation was taking place in Paris, the home of De Gaulle, and was drifting back and forth between the two languages that had come to symbolize our polarization. The girlfriend looked down at her hands and said nothing. The young man examined my face for a moment and then smiled.

"Maybe we will stay together. Who knows?"

I didn't ask him which way he would vote. We parted on friendly terms, and I went off in search of Tom. I felt I had done all I could for Canadian unity for one morning.

I was looking for an opportunity to experience Parisian nightlife and so leapt at the chance of a night cruise on the bateaux mouche with Tom and Anita, a fellow Canadian we had met at the hotel. We agreed to meet in front of Notre Dame at sunset.

The streets in front of the famous cathedral were lined with street performers and artists doing quick drawings for a few francs. I found Tom and Anita watching a puppet show with Jean, a Parisian friend of Anita's. Jean was a middle-aged realtor who looked like an oversized teddy bear with his well-stuffed paunch and fuzzy greying beard.

"*Bonjour*, Jean," I said in greeting. He smiled shyly through his beard and answered me in an indecipherable patter of French.

"Jean can't speak English," Anita offered. "We'll all just have to speak French tonight."

The thought of an entire evening spent speaking nothing but French was a bit daunting. My linguistic skills had come far, but not that far.

The sun dipped below the horizon in a sizzle of golden fire as we boarded our bateau mouche. We seated ourselves on the top deck of the converted barge, and the boat pushed off with a sibilant whoosh and floated down the Seine. Ahead of us was a flotilla of similar barges, bobbing in a tourist traffic jam.

"Quite romantic, isn't it?" Tom whispered in my ear.

I blushed and looked away from his penetrating gaze. This was ridiculous. We were good friends. Why ruin a perfectly good friendship by throwing a romance into it?

I laughed away his comment and spent the rest of the evening trying to ignore the warmth of his body next to mine.

Jean recommended an all-night jazz club as a fun way to finish off the evening. It was located in the Latin Quarter, just a short walk away from the bateaux mouche moorings.

Jean, obviously a regular, was greeted by the owner of the club with a shout of hello and a bear hug. He guided us past the small candle-lit tables of the restaurant and down stone steps into the dim interior of what had once been a wine cellar. It looked like a cave, with walls cut from wet, dark stone.

There was only enough space for two long tables that stretched the length of the low ceilinged room. A dwarf was singing a jazz version of "Feelings" on the stage, dramatically wiping the sweat from his brow with a handkerchief. We seated ourselves at the table and a waiter immediately appeared by our side.

"*Un pastis*," I ordered, having wanted to try this quintessentially French aperitif.

Tom decided to be adventurous and ordered the same. The pastis, milky and scented with anise, was better suited to the heat of Southern France but it added a continental touch to the evening.

The dwarf left the stage to a round of applause, and a bouncy Spanish woman vavoomed her way to the microphone. Her dark hair was swept up on top of her head, her ample figure squeezed into a red satin bustier dress. She was either a lounge singer or a prostitute who had made a wrong turn at the corner. A group of friends whooped loudly in the corner and shouted words of encouragement in Spanish.

The owner stepped up to the microphone and made a highly complimentary introduction. He could be forgiven for overstating her attributes a bit. What she lacked in finesse she made up for in gusto, belting out jazz numbers in a thick Spanish accent.

We were into the early hours of the morning before Anita glanced at her watch and made a gesture for us to go. Jean signalled for the bill and the owner dropped it before Anita with a smile and a "Bonsoir". I was half-way out of my seat when I noticed the look of horror on Anita's face.

"What is it? What's the matter?" I asked.

She gulped and looked up at me. "This bill is for seven hundred francs. That's well over one hundred dollars."

Jean looked at us curiously as we had shifted to English, and asked what the problem was.

Tom picked up the bill and looked at it. "Something must be wrong. We had eight drinks. It can't be fifteen bucks a drink."

Anita waved the owner over. He slid up to our side, oozing charm. "They must think we ordered a meal or something," Anita murmured to me, and then pointed her finger at the totalled bill.

The owner chuckled at our naiveté. "This cost is the cover charge, for the floor show." He pointed to a figure that equalled about fifteen dollars a head. With a hefty seven dollars a drink on top of that, we had each spent more on those few drinks than I had spent on food for two days.

Jean, seeing the distress on our faces, pulled out his wallet and pushed a wad of francs into the owner's hand. Tom made an effort to refuse, but Jean wouldn't hear of it. He felt responsible for not having warned us in advance.

Yet another pleasant Parisian. I was still waiting for the ogres of tourist lore to appear.

The next evening was my last in Paris. Tom and I had planned a romantic evening: two bottles of champagne to be consumed at the top of the Eiffel Tower. I had not been up the tower and thought this a suitable send-off for such a sensual city. I wanted to hang over the railings and bid a fond adieu to the twinkling lights of Paris below me.

I also wanted a romantic goodbye with Tom. I would be lying if I said I hadn't been aware of the change in our relationship. As my last day in Paris wound its way into a humid, star-sprinkled evening, I felt a sense of loss at the thought that Tom and I might not cross paths again.

We sat in my hotel room, looking out over the angled rooftops of Paris darkening in the sunset, and talked about our plans. There was a stillness in both of us, an unspoken sadness. First one bottle of champagne was opened, and then the other. We drank silently from chipped glasses and tried not to look at one another.

Tom took me in his arms for the first time as the warm, moist darkness of night settled over the city. I closed my eyes and felt his lips touch my own.

We never made it to the top of the Eiffel Tower.

xii a visit with jean vanier

I was almost sorry to arrive in the pretty northern town of Compiègne, best known as the location for the signing of the Armistice in 1918 as well as the location where a defeated France surrendered to Hitler in 1940. And yet I was there to complete an interview that I had been dreaming of since I began plotting out my itinerary in Canada. I had come to see Jean Vanier, the creator of the L'Arche communities for the mentally handicapped. Almost a hundred "arks" and thirty years later, his theories have influenced the way in which society views the mentally handicapped.

I was a fan, if such a word can be used in this context. I had been trying for weeks to wangle an interview, and had finally been squeezed into Jean's busy schedule at his original community at Trosly. I had even been invited for lunch. I should have been over the moon. But then, I was in love.

Tom and I had spent a romantic week wandering through the French countryside, filling in time before I was due to head north to Trosly. We hadn't a care in the world. But that was before we arrived in Compiègne.

I should preface this by saying that I have an overdeveloped conscience. I feel guilty if I squash a bug, let alone actually complete any major transgressions. And there I was, going to meet a man whom I respected, a one-time novitiate who lived his life as an example of Christian love and humility, while my lover waited for me in our hotel room in Compiègne. Stupid, I know. Especially for a grown woman who is not even Catholic. But I was a wreck.

I scuttled out of our hotel and walked hurriedly to the train station. A ride would be waiting there, so I had been told, to take me to Trosly. As I walked, I rummaged in my bag for my medicine vial. It contained a selection of aspirin and nausea tablets to combat any travel bugs, and a handful of tranquilizers in case of an emergency.

This was an emergency. I popped two tranquilizers into my mouth and counted off five minutes. Sweat was still trickling down my palms. The bloody things weren't working! I pulled out the bottle and popped in another pill, ignoring the sensible voice that was telling me that this was too high a dose, especially for someone who hadn't touched a tranquilizer in months.

As I neared the station, I could see a bespectacled, middle-aged man standing beside a beaten up Citroen with a small sign in his hand. It read L'Arche.

"Excuse me," I walked up to him, "Are you waiting for me? My name is Kim Herdman."

He nodded his head yes, and I noticed a desire to please in his blue eyes and the anxious angle of his jaw. "*Oui, oui.*" He smiled and patted at his chest. "*Je m'appelle Louis. Vous n'arrivez pas dans le train à Paris*?"

I shook my head no. "*Non, je suis arrivé hier.*"

"Ahh." Louis shrugged his shoulders in acceptance. He must have been around fifty, one of the many mentally handicapped adults who probably would have been institutionalized had it not been for Jean.

Louis deposited me with great care in the passenger seat of the dented car and we took off up the road out of Compiègne. Showing what I thought was suitably French discretion, I did not look up as we passed my hotel.

After a few introductory questions, I soon realized that Louis spoke only a rapid, rather garbled French that was difficult to understand. We slipped into a companionable silence.

We had just reached the outskirts of town when Louis suddenly slammed on the brakes.

"*Merde*!" he shouted and with a twist of the wheel skidded off the road onto a gravel patch. "*Je suis très stupide*!" He angrily slammed his hand against his forehead.

We sat there for a moment, dust rising around the wheels of the Citroen, while Louis conducted an angry conversation with himself.

I watched this with more than a little trepidation. "Louis? *Qu'est que le probleme*?"

For an answer, Louis grabbed the steering wheel and spun us back on to the road into Compiègne. He turned to me and blurted out an agitated, incomprehensible explanation.

It took me several minutes to discover that I was not the only person Louis was to pick up at the train station. In his nervousness at my early arrival, he had forgotten to wait for the other passengers.

The young man and woman were still waiting patiently for us in front of the station. Louis pulled up beside them and jumped out to repeat his agitated explanation. The man laughed and clapped him on the shoulder, dismissing Louis' dismay with a wave of his hand. The same hand was thrust through the car window to shake my own.

Pencil-thin but with a warm smile that seemed to add meat to his bones, he informed me that he was a priest who worked with the homeless in Paris. The woman worked for an organization that Jean had started called Faith and Light. She looked disapprovingly at my sleeveless cotton blouse and diaphanous skirt, prodding my conscience out of its momentary slumber.

I turned my attention to answering the priest's questions about my business with Jean.

"And what is the homeless situation like in France?" I asked after casting a nervous glance at the silent woman.

"It's getting worse. We don't have enough beds for them all, so we try to minister to them on the streets. But it's more than a warm bed: they need hope. It's a very difficult time." He was on his way to to chat with Jean about this and other problems.

The northern countryside outside of Compiegene thickened into lush dusky woods as we clocked up the kilometres towards Trosly. Louis appeared to have recovered from his earlier trauma and was humming happily as he drove. I nestled back comfortably in my seat. The sweat on my palms had disappeared and a calm warmth had spread its way across my stomach, a lovely narcotic sleepiness splashing around the edges. Even the quiet woman no longer bothered me.

These drugs are wonderful things, I thought naively to myself.

We motored into the village of Trosly just before lunch. When the first L'Arche community had opened there thirty years previously, it had consisted of one small house. The community had now all but taken over the town, utilising many of the grey stone buildings that lined the square.

We pulled through the gate of one of the larger houses into an expansive courtyard filled with milling people. The priest leaned forward and pointed to an open-air chapel that was set into one wing of the house. "This is L'Arche."

L'Arche. I paused and waited for a nervous fillip in my stomach. There was nothing. I sighed happily. This was going to be a breeze.

I clambered out of the Citroen and into the welcoming arms of a woman dressed in a flowing orange caftan.

"*Bonjour*," she said with a British accent. "You must be Kim."

I turned to wave goodbye to Louis. "Yes, I am. You must be the person whom I've been bothering with my telephone calls."

She gestured me into the L'Arche office with a swish of her caftaned arm. I had been expecting to see nuns and priests scuttling around in funereal black, but this woman seemed more like a sixty-year-old flower child. She looked as if she'd taken a left turn at Woodstock and kept right on going to France.

Her name was Clare and she briefed me on the day's events in a wood panelled office. I was going to attend chapel with the community and then have lunch at Jean's table.

"Jean's table?"

"Yes, that's right. We eat as a community here," she answered and then continued with the itinerary. After lunch, I could spend a short period of time chatting alone with Jean, before someone else from the community gave me a guided tour of the town. It sounded wonderful.

I had just begun to stand up when my knees suddenly buckled beneath me. I gripped the back of the chair for support and waited a moment for the spell to pass. The room was still rocking as Clare introduced me to a young woman from Puerto Rico. Maria's parents worked for Catholic charities in Puerto Rico and she spoke wonderful English. She was in her twenties and was spending a year working at L'Arche.

"Maria will take you to chapel and then on to lunch," Clare said.

I thanked Clare rather hoarsely and shakily followed Maria out into the courtyard. There was already quite a crowd in the chapel and all of the pews were filled. I was glad to sit down on anything, even if it was the balcony floor. The chapel, open on one side to the courtyard, was decorated in a natural, rustic style with old wood beams and a stone font. It struck me as warm and inviting, especially with so many young people sitting cross-legged on the floor around me.

"Our priest asked specially to come to L'Arche," Maria whispered as the service started.

I noticed that many of the servers were mentally handicapped residents of L'Arche. My gaze wandered around the congregation, at the able-bodied and at those who twitched and moaned uncontrollably in their seats. There was an air of joyful acceptance about the place. Unlike the institutions I had seen in Canada, L'Arche lacked that bitter smell that clings to the back of your throat: that mixture of industrial disinfectant and self-pity.

It was as they were lining up for communion that I spotted Jean for the first time.

"There he is," Maria whispered and pointed to a white haired man.

He was tall and thin, gangly is perhaps the best word, and dressed in a blue shirt and trousers. He looked rumpled, as if he hadn't bought new clothes in twenty years. When he bent over to receive communion, his body seemed to fold like a blue heron.

What profound destiny had brought him to such a place? I wondered as I watched him head back to his seat.

I already knew the facts: that when Vanier, the son of a Canadian Governor General, was studying at the Sorbonne a chance meeting with a local priest had brought the plight of two homeless mentally handicapped men to his attention. That was how L'Arche had begun, with Jean's efforts to provide a home to mentally handicapped adults. But how many of us would do the same thing? Offer up our secure lives to such a demanding fate?

The service ended and the crowd of a hundred or so filed out into the courtyard.

"Lunch is served in the main house," Maria said and led me inside.

It was an old farmhouse with cream walls and large airy rooms. People were everywhere, cooking lunch and setting the large communal tables that spread out from the kitchen through the dining rooms.

"This is Jean's table. Maybe I'll see you later," she said and disappeared into the steaming kitchen, leaving me standing awkwardly beside an empty table.

There was a rush of movement behind me as a large group of laughing people surged up to my table. "*Bonjour, bonjour*," they called out as if they had known me all their lives, and scraped back seats to sit down in.

I sat down myself, murmuring replies in quiet French. On my right, there sat a young man with Downe's syndrome. On my left was a young Frenchwoman who worked at Trosly. I chatted with both of them, trying in my rapidly worsening French to answer their questions.

"And you must be Kim," I heard a dry, powerful voice say from across the oval table. I looked up and saw that Jean had seated himself across from me, a smile creasing his long, academic face. "Do you speak French?"

I shook my head no. I was finding it difficult to understand the French used at L'Arche and preferred to plead ignorance of the language.

"Oh well. Here, Kim." He handed me a large bowl filled with tossed salad. "As our guest, you can start serving this. Everyone who comes to L'Arche is considered part of our community."

I accepted the bowl from him and began to dish out servings of salad to all seated around the table. Once I had finished my serving round, I sat down and helped myself to some bread. Jean was busy chatting with two people seated beside him, so I asked the young Frenchwoman about her life at Trosly.

"I love it," she answered in thickly accented English, her face glowing with a radiance I envied.

I could understand the pull of this place, the sense of belonging, of commitment. I took a quick sip of water. I couldn't think like that. If I did, I might never make it back to Compiègne.

I took another sip of water and felt its coolness travel refreshingly down my throat. I wished I could splash some on my warm face, if only to stop my eyelashes from drifting down to rest on my cheeks. If I wasn't careful, I was going to land head first on my dinner plate, snoring soundly into the asparagus.

And what was even stranger, I didn't care. The drugs had not merely destroyed my nervousness about the interview, but had dissolved all my inhibitions as well. What was wrong with having a nap in the bread dish? After all, we're just one big happy family, aren't we?

A slam of a fist on the table beside me roused me back into a semi-conscious state. The young man with Downe's syndrome wanted me to pour him some water. Thankful for a task, I splashed some water into his glass and then watched owlishly as he drank it. I don't think he was particularly impressed with my performance, as he asked his other dinner partner to assist him with his bread.

It was a smart move.

Lunch was finally concluded amongst the dull roar of a hundred conversations and the clattering of gravy-stained plates. I offered to help with the clean up, but gentle hands laughingly refused my offer and pointed me in the direction of a small anteroom. Jean was waiting for me.

I picked up my bag and, with a definite list to my walk, headed towards the open door. I have no idea what I looked like, but I felt like I was walking uphill in cement shoes. The door was in front of me, I could even see Jean waiting for me on the window seat, and yet it seemed to take forever for me to reach him.

Life was getting very strange.

As I found out afterwards, one of the after-effects of the massive dose of drugs I had taken is periodic blackouts. I suppose that is why the rest of my time at L'Arche seems to swim in and out of my memory with the artistic fuzziness of a European movie. Luckily, for both me and my editors, I do remember some of the interview. I was also able to take notes, written in a hand very much like the signature I used when my right hand was encased in a plaster cast. Decipherable, but only just.

I do remember sitting beside Jean on the cushioned window seat and asking him some introductory questions about himself and L'Arche.

"That's been written about before," he said brusquely and waved away any further questions I had about his history. "We have all sorts of papers on how it was started. You can get some at the office before you go."

I was taken aback. Not only had Jean disrupted the flow of the interview, but he had displayed a side to his personality that I had not expected. I had imagined a man oozing warmth and a transcendental calm. This person showed both impatience and a temper.

I scrabbled around in my drugged mind for some other questions. "How do you think society in general treats the mentally handicapped?"

He paused, concentrating on the question. "It's more a question of how we can create communities that welcome differences." He paused and then answered his own question. "Don't hide your weaknesses. We have to respect these differences and offer a community that is a place for both love and growth."

"What is life like for you here in Trosly?"

A smile softened his lean face. What I had taken for gruffness seemed more impatience than unkindness. "We live a continual miracle here, you know. It's wonderful."

"What about other social issues, such as homelessness? Abuse? What are your feelings about these problems? You have done wonderful things in showing society how to live with the mentally handicapped. Can society solve these other problems?"

"It's the same really. No matter what the issue. We use violence in the same way that we don't give bread to the hungry: it's refusing to care."

As the interview progressed, I began to see that perfection was not what I should have been seeking in this meeting. The qualities I had admired in Jean were not found in perfect people, but rather in ordinary people rising above their own pain to help others.

My actual memory of the discussion about L'Arche dims at this point, the only evidence that it occurred is to be found in my notes. Memory splashes back in brief and embarrassing patches. I remember holding Jean's hand at some point in the interview and spilling out my confusion about my writing and the direction I was taking in my life with Tom. I can also remember his calm and rather overwhelmed reply: "God guides us all".

Blackness, thankfully, blocks out the rest of that conversation.

A young woman was waiting to take me on a tour of Trosly after I finished my interview with Jean. I don't remember her name or where she came from. I can only say that she was young and spoke English and made a brave attempt to pretend that there was nothing wrong with me.

Somehow we made it through the short tour with me staggering along the tiny lanes. She brought me back to one of the cottages that served as a dorm and with typical kindness tucked me up in her own bed. I slept in a drugged state for the rest of the day.

She woke me at dinnertime and deposited me with great tact into the back of the Citroen. Not even Louis asked any embarrassing questions. I think I pleaded travel exhaustion, or perhaps a tropical illness. Malaria or something. I'm sure I didn't fool anyone. In fact, I wouldn't blame them if they had taken a whiff of my breath as I lay snoring for four hours in that dorm room.

In the months following this incident, I have often wondered what Jean thought of this meeting, of this strange journalist who turned an interview into a rambling confession before collapsing in a comatose heap in one of his dorms. Did he think I was a lush? Or just a confused person looking for some guidance?

I sincerely hope that whatever he remembers of this, if he remembers it at all, is touched with some Christian kindness and forgiveness.

Knowing Jean Vanier, I'm sure it is.

xiii train travels through Germany, Switzerland, and almost Czechoslovakia ❖❖

Berlin seemed the obvious place for a story on the new Europe. The wall was down and tourists were flooding in to experience the Alice in Wonderland like flavour of the dual cities rejoined.

With a bit of last minute juggling, Tom and I managed to book a reservation on the night train from Amsterdam to Berlin: two sleeper seats in a first class carriage. Our first hint that this was going to be an unusual trip was the sight of the platform as we disembarked outside of Amsterdam to catch our connecting train to Germany.

"All these people can't be going to Germany, can they?" Tom whispered as we pushed our way through a morass of dread-locked teenagers.

Young backpackers were nothing new to us, but this crowd had a fashion sense all its own. Instead of hiking packs, they carried by an assortment of ratty army surplus bags with dirty underwear destined for laboratory experiments poking out of their top pockets. Their tie-dyed t-shirts proclaimed a new Woodstock generation, only this time without the benefit of communual washing.

A train shooshed up to the platform in a hiss of steam while a loudspeaker voice announced its destination: Czechoslovakia. We waited with bated breath. Surely a huge chunk of this crowd would be going to Prague?

"They're not leaving," Tom muttered dismally as a few hardy souls pushed out of the crowd to board the train. We watched as the rest merely shifted on their tattered sacks and lit another joint.

Our train was next up the track. Sure enough, the crowd stood up as if from some silent signal, shook itself in a single body, and heaved towards the edge of the cement siding.

"Look at them. It's like bargain day at K-Mart," I said.

"It's okay. They'll all be going second class."

What we didn't realize was that the train was so overbooked that any space, whatever class, was fair game. The aisles of our first class carriage were clogged with young bodies stretched out in their sleeping bags like miners protecting a claim.

"I don't know where to step," I said, gingerly trying to avoid outstretched arms.

"Watch out for faces. As for the rest, they can live without the odd finger."

We finally uncovered our cabin. The compartment was filled, and it took a few minutes of bickering before we roused two Japanese girls from our reserved seats. We sat down with a sigh of relief and examined our compartment mates. A middle-aged American couple were pressed against the window, experiencing the novelty of European train travel for the first time.

"Our travel agent recommended it," the woman said, looking sheepishly at the bulk of humanity piling up outside our cabin door. "She said it was the only way to travel."

The husband snorted at this comment. For him at least, the adventure appeared to be paling rapidly.

Seated across from Tom and I was a Dutch woman and her mentally handicapped son. The woman was in her seventies and looked far too frail for such a venture. Her middle-aged son sat stolidly beside her, his hair sleeked back, his dark suit and slim tie chosen with the sensible 1950's style of his elderly mother. His heavy-lidded eyes swam vacantly towards us before being distracted by the glass cabin doors and the crowds outside.

Time passed fitfully. Conversation petered out, and the American couple opted for sleeping away their European experience. We decided that this was the best bet and I made a half-hearted attempt to curl up against Tom's shoulder. The early evening light drifted into darkness as we moved rhythmically towards Germany.

Somewhere around the German border, I was roused by the whistle of the train pulling into a station. Across from me in the darkened cabin, I could see a glowing red light, like a firefly. I sat up straighter and saw that the Dutch man was smoking a cigar, puffing on it like a bellows and blowing the smoke out the open cabin doors. The young men outside were passing around a bottle, and I could hear the subway-like shuffle of people climbing on and off the train. Down the aisle, I heard a tuneless strum on a steel-stringed guitar and a Jamaican voice say, "Hey man, do you want to sing something?"

The train started up with a shudder and, as if in reply, a chorus of ragged, drunken voices picked up a refrain.

"Roll out the barrel, we'll have a barrel of fun ..."

Tom groggily sat up. "What the hell's that?"

"I'd vote for Saturday night at the Elephant and Castle."

Our pub choir continued to greet each departure with the same chorus. By the early hours, their chant had slipped into a drunken mumble, spotted with half hearted "Rulls out th' barrul." Sometimes they would miss a departure entirely and there would be a frantic refrain as the train pulled out of the station. In between stations, our Rasta friend continued the musical entertainment by strumming away on his guitar and pretending that he was warming up for Top of the Pops.

Somewhere around Leipzig, I gave up on the idea of sleep altogether and contented myself with watching the landscape flit darkly past the window. I felt a growing unease at the thought of being in Germany, something which I dismissed as paranoia. Too many black and white movies with Nazis hovering malevolently in leather overcoats. I mean, the war was water long under the bridge. Maybe if I was Jewish ... But I wasn't, so there went that excuse.

But somehow that couldn't stop the chill that was spreading through my body. In the stillness as we slid into each station, I could see empty trains sitting idly along the tracks, lit by the institutional glare of the white floodlights. And all I could think of was barbed wire and the millions of bodies.

I was shivering when Tom awoke. He looked out into the flourescent-tinged gloom and shook his head at my fears. "It was over a long time ago," he said gently and held me tighter in his arms.

"I know. It's just that I see their faces looking out at me."

Nature calls, at least with me, at the most inappropriate times. Dawn was just breaking through the clouds as I roused Tom from his prone position across my lap and informed him that I was off to the bathroom.

"Fine. Just don't fall off the train," was his mumbled reply.

The Dutch man had finished his cigar by this time and was happily humming a song.

"*Guten Morgen*," I said and stepped over his outstretched legs.

The aisle outside looked like a bomb shelter. Bodies in varying stages of unconsciousness were strewn across the floor. Remembering Tom's dictum about avoiding important organs, I moved from one thigh to another like stepping stones. Even entering the bathroom was a battle as I had to dislodge the young woman who had chosen to wedge herself into the doorway to sleep.

I was exhausted by the time I returned to the cabin. The entire trip had become more like orienteering than travel. I stumbled over the last few bodies and fell headlong into my seat. Unfortunately, Tom was already occupying it.

"You made it back," he said in muffled tones from beneath my chest.

"Yes, but who knows what internal damage I've done to those poor people to get back here."

Tom sat up and blinked in the greyish morning light before staring in some consternation at the base of the cabin door. A large foot was sticking through it. At one time it must have been enclosed in a sneaker, but time had long since disintegrated the shoe into a rotting, odiferous blend of canvas and rubber.

"I must have knocked it in when I fell," I said.

Tom leaned over and examined the foot with pinched nostrils. The smell was horrid. "I don't care how it got in here. I just want it out."

He tried to nudge it out the door, but the foot clung tenaciously to its new location as if its sole was laced with cement. A half-hearted attempt to wake up the owner also failed. With an angry swipe, Tom grabbed the mud-spattered pant leg and threw the foot out the door. We both watched as it came to a thudding landing outside. No one moved. Not the owner. Not even the poor young man whose right arm was clobbered with it.

"Do you think they're dead?" Tom asked.

"I don't know. I think it's more like a temporary condition. They'll rise from the dead when we get to the station." I paused as inspiration struck. "We should call them Lazarus."

Our somnolent zombie friends were immediately christened the Lazaruses. Their ability to sleep through everything was miraculous, to say the least. They even managed to sleep through our arrival at the Zoo Bahnhof and the disembarkation of all the train's other passengers. With a spasm of pity, I jumped back on the train and attempted to wake one of them. It was only after I slapped him hard on the face that his eyes blearily opened.

"Whaaatt issth itt?"

"You're in Berlin," I said. "You've got to get up."

He looked surprised, then happy, before he closed his eyes once again. I left him to the mercy of the German train system.

Berlin was as cynical and cold as I had expected it to be hopeful and welcoming. This city of rebirth was suffering from postpartum depression: an influx of refugees and tourists as well as the economic costs of reuniting all seemed to make the cultured citizens of Berlin hard and unpleasant. I'd found the *zeitgeist* amongst the rubble of the wall, and I didn't like it.

In some ways, it was as if my nightmarish visions on that train ride continued to plague me throughout Berlin. As we finally left the city, a flurry of spray-painted swastikas grabbed my attention through the dusty window of our taxi. But there was something else there too, something perhaps more symbolic of the conflict between the past and present, between the new Germany and the old. Another, hopefully more representative, artist had attempted to obliterate the swastikas with spray-painted letters. *Nazi Raus*, they said.

Nazis out.

* * *

The train from Vienna to Zurich was a swiss one - fast, spotless and expensive. In our cabin, a middle-aged businessman was already engrossed in his copy of the *International Herald Tribune*. A single woman sat in a corner seat reading a German paperback.

I had just pulled out a crossword puzzle when the cabin door slid open and a blonde haired man tumbled in. His bronzed body was clad in a brightly-coloured pair of shorts and a t-shirt emblazoned with an image of Michelangelo's David. A thick, perfumed cloud of Aramis followed him in.

"Are these seats empty?" he asked in a loud Texas twang blended with a distinct feminine lisp that dragged the businessman out from behind his newspaper.

"No, they're free," I answered.

He flopped his backpack onto the shelf above me. "Randy," he called out into the hallway, "There are some lovely seats in here."

Randy appeared with a similar backpack straining from his shoulders. He was as good-looking as our bronzed cabin mate, although with neatly coiffed dark hair.

"Fantastic," Randy sighed and piled his belongings onto the other luggage rack before collapsing in a seat.

The blonde man plopped down into the seat beside me and smiled in a friendly fashion. I smiled in return and introduced myself and Tom.

"Hi there. I'm Mike and this is Randy. We're from Fort Worth. Texas."

"Have you been in Europe very long?" I asked and turned to find that Tom had buried himself in the crossword puzzle, a definite humourous crook to his mouth.

"Ohhhh," Mike exhaled with orgasmic enthusiasm. "It's been three weeks now." I looked with a mixture of disbelief and awe at the neatly pressed pleats in his shorts. "And it's been wonderful. We've been all over Italy and Austria. Milan, Florence, Vienna."

"Vienna, I LOVE Vienna," Randy inserted. "I could live there, you know."

I somehow couldn't picture Randy sipping coffee and nibbling a sacher torte at a street cafe. His face was pressed against the glass partition sep-arating our cabin from the hallway, his mouth making occasional oohing sounds at the scenery.

"Yes, it's quite nice there. Did you two like Italy? We're headed there now."

"It was beautiful, but it was so dirty and hot. I mean, we're used to hot. Fort Worth gets hot. But all that dirt on the streets..." Mike shriveled up his nose like an insulted rabbit. "But Rome was wonderful. We went to a Sunday service at the Vatican. It was just, just," Mike seemed to be searching for further superlatives, "fabulous."

My estimation of the two of them rose a few notches. "I'd love to attend a church service in Europe, but I'm too afraid to go. It's the language problem. You know, I'd stand up when everyone else was sitting down. I wouldn't really understand what was going on."

Randy turned his attention to us briefly. "No, they were very helpful to us. We just followed everyone else, you know, and they showed us what to do. They knew we couldn't speak Italian, so they kind of nudged us when we were supposed to take the bread and wine. It was almost like church at home."

I looked from Randy, who was once again staring out the window, to Mike's beaming face. "You took communion?"

"Oh yeah. Everyone else was."

"Are you Catholic?"

Mike leaned back in surprise, as if Catholics were as few on the ground in Fort Worth as vegetarians. "No, we're Methodist." He paused at my horrified stare and attempted to reassure me. "Don't worry, we're Christians. We take communion all the time at home."

"But you don't understand. You can't take communion in a Catholic church unless you're Catholic. Especially not at St. Peters!"

Mike patted me gently on the shoulder. "I'm sure they didn't mind. It's all the same God after all."

I turned to look at Tom. He was now almost buried behind the crossword and I thought I could detect a slight hiccuping sound. The businessman had given up on his newspaper and was openly listening to our conversation with a bemused fascination. Only the German woman seemed oblivious.

Lunchtime arrived and with it the ritual opening of packed lunches. There is something about the sharing of food with strangers that forges friendship. Within five minutes, the two Europeans in our cabin were nibbling away at our Salzburg salamis and rolls and chatting away pleasantly. The single woman, it turned out, was from Vienna. She spoke a crisp, clean English that made her the focus for Randy's unending questions about life in Vienna.

"And how much would it cost to buy an apartment there?" I could hear him asking her over the munching of sausages. Randy appeared to be a great one for buying real estate. "I'm also really interested in getting some property in the countryside." There was the crinkling of a potato chip bag. "It's *soooo* beautiful here."

The businessman was not so easily deciphered. He was from Moonsee, a beautiful village outside of Salzburg, but also said he had homes all over the world. I put this down to exaggeration until he displayed a geographical knowledge that included not only major European cities, but also the tiniest towns in my own province of British Columbia. His grasp of world politics was also tinged with the feel of an insider. I tried to find out exactly what his business was, but he expertly sidestepped my questions. He sat across from me with a small, knowing grin spread across his face, as smart and slippery as his expensive gucci loafers.

By mid-afternoon, we had slipped over the border into Switzerland. The mountains of Austria had become the alpine peaks of children's storybooks. Randy was in seventh heaven, pressed against the window outside the compartment with his camera at his side.

Mike, however, was more interested in telling me about his dacshund, Candy, and her recent traumatic illness.

"She was in such pain. We didn't know what was the matter." He was almost tearing up at the thought. "She just lay there, crying."

Tom stood by the window with Randy, answering his questions about Canada. Europe had obviously widened Randy's horizons. He was considering Canada as a viable real estate alternative if moving to Austria didn't pan out.

"And then they told us they'd have to operate. Back surgery." Mike paused dramatically; the businessman and I leaned forward expectantly in our seats. "We didn't know for twenty-four hours whether she was going to walk again. She just lay there in her bandages on the blanket. And then," he choked up momentarily, "she staggered to her feet. It was a miracle."

Even I had to wipe away a stray tear. The businessman sniffled quietly. Mike pulled out his wallet and showed us a series of post-op pictures of Candy and her soul mate, Randy's dachshund, Amber.

Tom peered in the door, looking for an excuse to escape Randy's questions. He saw the three of us sniffling over dog pictures and retreated quickly back out into the hall.

"Mike, you're missing all of these beautiful mountains," Randy called in.

Mike waved Randy away with a flutter of his hand and brought out a new assortment of dog pictures.

"But Mike," Randy continued, "these are fantastic. You're never going to get another chance to see mountains like this." Randy paused and turned to Tom. "You have mountains like this in Canada, don't you?"

Tom nodded yes.

"How much would one of those peaks cost me in Canada?"

* * *

Czechoslovakia. The name brought with it images of Wenceslaus Square and snow drifting over the fairytale spires of cathedrals; of cold pilsener and the faint strains of a distant Danube waltz. But it also revived memories of the grey march of communism and the crushing of the Prague Spring. I sat in the Vienna Banhof, an open guidebook on my lap, my finger tracing the vein like curls of the Danube as it drifted into Czechoslovakia. Tom was off in search of food and water, leaving me to choose our next destination.

What was it to be? Hungary or Czechoslovakia? Tom was voting for Hungary, but my heart was hankering after the beauty of Prague. According to the guidebook, Canadians no longer needed visas to get into newly independent Czechoslovakia. Hungary still required them, which meant an extra night in Vienna and a trip to the embassy the next morning.

That settled it. It was going to be Czechoslovakia or bust.

It was nearing midnight by the time we boarded the Vienna - Berlin train, which stopped in Prague on its way to eastern Germany.

"Oh no, Kim, we're going back to Berlin!" Tom whispered in mock horror as we clambered into our cabin.

He had no idea how soon we would be wishing for just such luck.

We immediately staked out our seats, having learned a lesson from our last overnight trip, and settled down to sleep through to Prague. The young Berliners in our cabin did the same. I had been asleep for about an hour when I heard the cabin door slide open and felt a hand shaking me on the shoulder.

"*Gute nacht*."

I opened my eyes, blinking against the amber glare of the station floodlights. A soldier stood above me. He was wearing a grey felt trenchcoat belted at the waist, the thick leather covered with military insignias and, most frightening of all, a gun. I shot up in my seat, shaking Tom awake at the same time.

"Passport," said the soldier with a brusque manner that was more businesslike than threatening.

"*Ja, Ja*," I said, slipping into my weak German. I fumbled in my money belt for my passport, all the time whispering angrily to Tom. "Wake up, Tom. For God's sake, the bloody KGB is here."

Tom sat up blearily, his eyes focusing on the soldier with a mixture of surprise and disbelief. "Hello, ahh, *Gute nacht*," he murmured and turned his attention to my efforts to retrieve our passports. "Are we at the border already?"

I gave him what I hoped was a quelling glance. "Yes. Where the hell do you think we are, Monte Carlo?"

I handed the soldier our passports, and he rapidly flipped through them. "Canada," he murmured and then continued in a thick accent, "Visas? You have no visas?"

"Visas? No, we read that we didn't have to have visas," Tom answered. "Canadians and EEC countries don't need them."

The soldier looked at us for a moment, shook his head abruptly, and then handed us back our passports. "Off," he said. He then reached past us for the Berliners' passports and flipped through them hurriedly.

"Off?" we echoed.

"Off." It was a sudden Slavic exhalation. "Off train now." And with that he handed back the German passports and headed down the hallway.

Tom and I looked at each other in disbelief. One minute we had been peacefully sleeping our way to Prague, the next minute we were being unceremoniously booted off the train. "I'll go and deal with him," I said, leaping to my feet. "You get the bags ready just in case." And with that I took off down the hallway at a run.

I caught up with him in the next carriage, working his way through a mass of German passports.

"Excuse me. I'm the Canadian you said had to get off the train?"

He looked over at me and sighed. "*Ja.*"

"Is it possible for us to stay on the train and get our visas at Prague?"

"No," he answered curtly and moved on to the next cabin. I followed doggedly behind.

"Okay, can we just stay on the train and get off at Berlin?"

He murmured good evening to the people in the cabin and collected their passports.

"No." He turned and looked at me directly. His English was bad, but not so bad that I couldn't understand his message. "No visa, you cannot enter Czechoslovakia. These your choices. You get off train now, by yourself, yes? If no, I throw you off train now. If you hide on train, someone arrest you in Prague. Okay?"

And with a nod, he left that cabin and headed for the next. He was almost at the last carriage, and therefore at the end of our time to leave the train without assistance. I raced down the hallway, pushing past the groups of young men who were hanging out the windows.

"Tom," I shouted before I had even reached our cabin, "We've got to get off the train now!"

Tom was already two steps ahead of me and had our bags stacked beside the exit door. As the train started to inch forward, he threw our bags onto the platform and jumped out after them.

"C'mon, Kim. Jump," he called out. I leapt down onto the cement siding as the train slowly began to chug its way out of Austrian territory.

"*Auf Wiedersehen*!" a chorus of male voices shouted derisively from the windows, and I made a weak gesture of waving.

I listened to their laughter as the white lights of the train disappeared over the border.

I now know where the loneliest place on earth is. It is the Austrian-Czech border at two o' clock in the morning.

"Where are we?" I asked plaintively as the train's chugging dissipated into silence.

Tom pointed to a sign on the wall. "Gmund."

"Gmund. Wonderful. And when can we get out of Gmund?"

"As far as the schedule is concerned, seven in the morning."

"Lovely. And what are we supposed to do until then?"

Tom put the schedule away in his backpack and watched as I walked angrily up and down the siding. "I think waiting for the train might be a good idea," he answered sharply.

I spun around on my heel, prepared for an argument, when a movement off to the side of the platform caught my eye. I leapt to Tom's side as if I had been yanked there by an invisible string.

"Who is it?" I whispered.

"How the hell am I supposed to know?"

Out of the gloom, two figures materialized on the other side of the tracks. They were dressed in the typical Eastern European uniform of grey greatcoat and peaked cap. As they neared us, I realized that one of them was the same soldier I had spoken to on the train.

"Hello," the soldier said and came to a stop ten feet away from us. They were still on the outskirts of the floodlight beam, which cast their features into shadow.

"*Gute nacht*," Tom answered.

There was a moment's silence as we examined each other: Tom and I standing stock still in the glare of the station lights, the two of them standing in the shadows on the opposite side of the tracks. The unfamiliar soldier took a step towards us, and we involuntarily stepped away.

"Where you going?" he asked in rough English.

What did he mean, where were we going? Did he think we were plotting to make a break for Prague on foot?

"Vienna?" I answered hesitantly.

"No, now. Where you going now!" In his attempt to speak more clearly, he barked out the question. Tom and I jumped closer together.

This was like something from the Cold War. Our parents would know nothing until the consul contacted them with the news that we'd been sent off to a gulag. I looked out into the gloom surrounding us, at the fields and wired fences.

"Where is Czechoslovakia?"

The soldier pointed left.

I pointed right. "Then that's where we're going."

There was a pause and then I thought I saw a flicker of a smile flit across the face of the soldier I had met before. He took a sudden leap over the tracks and was up on the siding beside us. The other soldier followed him, his coat flapping in loose felt folds around his legs.

"You sleep?" my soldier said.

I paused at this tricky question. Did they want to know whether we slept in the West? Or was there something vaguely sexual involved here? "I'm sorry. I don't understand."

"Sleep. Sleep." He paused and looked in some consternation at the other soldier. They had a brief chat in Czech and then turned to us. "You sleep here. Night. *Nacht*. Now."

The other soldier went to a darkened empty train that was sitting at the siding and banged on a door until it opened. He then pointed inside and made a pantomime gesture of sleeping.

"You want us to sleep in the train tonight?" I asked, and he smiled and nodded his head rapidly.

"Yes. Vienna train. Morning."

"This is the train we're supposed to take tomorrow morning. *Danke*," Tom replied warmly.

"Sleep good," my soldier said.

"Yes, you too," Tom added.

We paused, and in that moment I saw that there wasn't that much difference between East and West. On the surface we were the typical wealthy Western tourists, and they the grey-toned agents of Eastern oppression. But we all just wanted a good night's sleep.

"*Gute nacht*," they said, and with a smile and a nod the two of them disappeared into the darkness.

Days later, we finally picked up a newspaper and saw the shocking headlines about a Soviet putsch. While we had been shakily cementing East-West relations in Gmund, a coup was being plotted in Moscow.

Communism was dead. The red menace had fallen with a swiftness that was stunning for such a lethargic, overgrown beast. The world had changed, and we hadn't even known it. How ironic that we should have shared such a moment in history stuck on the border with two communist border guards.

And yet how right.

xiv gelato with the pope ❖❖❖❖❖❖❖❖

I had arrived, with Tom in tow, to write about the Vatican - not the well touristed exterior, but the real world that is locked away from the public. I wanted into the real thing, the real Vatican. The fact that the heat of the August sun had driven most Romans to the seaside didn't deter me. The reality that business as usual in August is as foreign to Italians as a long-term presidency or paying income tax barely fazed me. I had the bit between my teeth. I was going to get into the Vatican.

Give up, Kim." Tom took a slow sip of his caffe latte and gazed at me through half-closed eyes. He was trying out his Marcello Mastroianni look.

"Give up! I'm not going to give up. So what if I can't get anyone in the Vatican to answer my messages." I took a determined bite out of an almond biscotti, crisp and buttery. "So what if I can't even find a single person who is still working in this city." Another vicious bite followed by a slurp of cappuccino. "Does that mean I should give up?"

"Yes, it does. You can't get anyone in this entire city to pick up the bloody phone, let alone answer a message. No one is here, Kim. They've left the city to us, the rampaging tourist masses, and gone to the beach."

"Alright then." I slammed my glass mug down on the counter of the packed coffee bar. "We'll just have to go in person. C'mon. Drink up. The Vatican awaits us."

We crossed the street to Termini Station, the main train and subway station in Rome. After buying our subway ticket from a tobacconist, an interesting Italian business arrangement, we headed down the cement steps that lead into its dungeon-like interior. The platform itself looked like a crumbling set from a World War II film - a bunker in which *Il Duce* hides himself from the bloodthirsty mobs. Beautiful Roman teenagers lounged with tanned grace and linen perfection against rotting pillars. American tourists in I LOVE NY baseball caps and Renaissance art t-shirts huddled like startled sheep next to the tracks.

A train pulled into the station with a rush of warm air, and the Romans stirred expectantly. The subway doors hissed open and there was a brief pause as shopping bags were picked up and luggage rearranged. Suddenly, I felt a gust of hot air come from behind me as a crowd of people rushed forward, propelling me to the side and away from the doors in a triumphant whoosh. Romans, old, young, fat, thin, pushed past me in a solid, trampling wall of flesh.

I saw Tom disappear behind the girth of an immense Italian woman, who was brandishing her grocery bag as if it were a bayonette. Two young girls, who couldn't have been more than twelve, elbowed me out of the way with a finesse that would have been greatly appreciated in the World Wrestling Federation. The only ones left standing on the platform as the dust cleared were Tom and I and a group of stunned tourists. A woman in a Da Vinci repro t-shirt looked like she was about to cry.

"Are you alright?" Tom asked as we boarded the car.

"Yeah, fine. Just a little shaken up, that's all."

I looked at the Romans seated around us. It was as if the stampede I had just witnessed had never occurred. The two girls were once again innocent youngsters, singing to themselves. The Roman housewife with the grocery bag looked as if she had never manhandled anything more lethal than a manicotti.

The train started up and trundled along with a chuggedy-chuggedy clacking to the next stop. This time I had enough sense to get out of the way before the subway doors opened.

The rush of air as warm bodies stormed onto the train hit me like a physical blow. People dove at empty seats with the desperation of famine victims lunging at a last crust of bread. A group of children flung themselves simultaneously at a row of seats, ending up topsy-turvy on top of one another.

"Hey, watch out!" Tom shouted at one overly enthusiastic teenager who sideswiped him as he made a rugby lunge at the last seat. The boy's sweaty, chagrined expression probably had more to do with having lost the seat to a businessman who'd slapped his bottom into it a second earlier, than any regret for the pale bruises Tom was to carry on his ribcage for the next few days.

"Why do they do it?" Tom asked when we finally emerged near the Vatican. "Some of them only went a stop or two, and yet they fought for a seat as if this was the second battle of Anzio."

I shrugged my shoulders. I didn't understand the Italian psyche any more than he did. And if I couldn't understand Italians, how on earth was I going to get in to see the Pope?

"Gelato. Pineapple. Oooh. Pineapple and Peach. Mmmmm. Doesn't that sound good? Maybe some lemon, too."

We had stopped at a small *gelateria* beside the Vatican. Tom stared at me with the same expression fathers-to-be exhibit towards pregnant wives. One part affection. Two parts exasperation.

"Pick a flavour, Kim."

I stared at the metal containers crammed with a rainbow of rich, deep framboises and mud-dark mochas.

"Pineapple. No, melon. No. Ummm,"

"*Uno melone e uno mocha,*" Tom supplied for both of us.

"But I wanted more than one flavour," I whined as we walked out onto the piping hot street.

"You sound like a six-year-old." Tom took a sideways lick at his dripping cone, looking hardly more than ten himself.

"I know. It's an addiction. I eat ice cream and I'm a kid again. Except this isn't just ice cream. This is heaven."

"This is gelati."

"I know. Maybe I should forget about writing about the Vatican and just write about the ice cream."

With a sloppy chocolate kiss, Tom waved me off in the direction of the first Vatican gate. "You're the one who said you could get into the Vatican. I'm off to the museum. Don't get into trouble. And if you get in, remember: play nice and share your gelato with the Pope."

I entered Vatican City without the faintest idea of how I was going to get into the inner sanctum. All tourist traffic was kept well in check by the Swiss Guards, the elaborately-uniformed personal bodyguards of the Pope. Their purpose in life was to keep the Pope in and me out. Skulking like a bad Eastern European spy, I hovered near the gate. How could I get in there without a pass? I searched my brain for something, anything that a journalist would do in this situation. There was only one option. I was going to have to sneak in.

Few people seemed to be using the gate. A priest, his black soutane flapping around his knees like a buttoned-up overcoat, passed by me carrying a heavy leather folder. He nodded to the Swiss Guard and stepped through. Summoning up a similar air of self-importance, I followed quickly in his footsteps.

A rush of gold, red and blue fabric materialized in front of me, blocking my path. "*Bongiorno.*"

I looked up at a mammoth Swiss Alp of a man, whose masculinity was not even dented by the rather ridiculous costume he was wearing. Pretend deafness? No. Perhaps plead ignorance of Italian? But what language to speak? He might, after all, know English.

"*Pardon, je ne parle pas Italienne. Je veux aller la Vatican pour mon travaille. Je suis une journaliste*." With a suitably Gallic smile, I attempted to step past him.

"*Votre passe, mademoiselle*?" He stopped me with an outstretched hand, all the time staring pointedly at my gelato which was now dripping down towards his lovely toe shoes.

"*Passe*?" I said with what I hoped was charming surprise.

Thick as a cuckoo clock, he was not.

I was spun around and sulked my way back down the clogged path to St. Peters. Why didn't I think that he would speak French? After all, where did I think he came from? Inner Mongolia?

I wandered through the magnificent collonade that encircles St. Peters, untouched by the pageantry of history around me. My melone gelato offered minimal comfort. Fighting the crowds, the heat, and the bureaucracy of a European summer was becoming too much. I took another mournful slurp of my gelato. Why not trash the job and just vegetate on some nice Greek island for a month? Another slurp. Either that or go and work in a *gelateria* for the rest of the summer.

The flash of a tourist information sign caught my attention. My spirits lifting marginally, I headed across the square and down the steps into a darkened room. It was filled with camera-bedecked tourists buying Vatican paraphernalia. A nun sat behind a desk calmly watching them, her veil settled with the comfort of long use around her aging, kindly face.

She stood up and walked to the counter as if drawn by my obvious unhappiness. "Yes, Dear. Can I help you?" she offered in a comforting Irish accent.

I explained my plight.

"I see. A journalist wanting to write about the Vatican. How interesting." She smiled with such ingenuous calm that I wished I had finished my ice cream first. I licked quickly to stop a puddle from forming on the floor by my feet. “You’ll be wanting someone in the press office then?”

My heart bounded upward in an athletic leap. “Yes, I would, thanks. If that’s alright?”

“Certainly. I’ll get the address and a map for you.”

“Is the press office in the Vatican?” I asked and pointed towards one of the gates. “You know, through there?”

“Yes.” Her gnarled hands pulled out a map from beneath the counter and pointed to an X on a section of the privileged interior buildings.

I felt an almost suicidal urge to stop her. This was too easy. Didn’t she know she shouldn’t be giving out this information? What if I was an assassin?

“This is the press office here,” she continued. “And this is the name of the person you should speak to.” A piece of Vatican stationery and a firm hand etched out a woman’s name and address.

I grasped the paper in my hand, as if unable to believe in its existence.

“Thank you,” I stuttered. “I mean, really, thank you.”

“That’s alright, Dear. Go with God.”

With the paper in one hand and ice cream in the other, I could have kissed her.

Not wanting to lose the momentum of my sudden run of good luck, I pushed through a crowd of tourists and pilgrims snapping photographs of the Swiss Guards and walked out into a kind of No Man’s Land surrounding the gate. I walked directly up to the first guard I saw. He swiveled to look at me, his fifteenth-century axe planted firmly on the ground. He did not bother to conceal his surprise at my appearance, which still included my dripping gelato.

I took a deep breath. I still might not get through. A nun’s note was only marginally better than nothing at all.

“Good morning.”

“*Bongiorno*,” the guard replied. He didn’t seem as physically intimidating as the previous guard, with a gentle face and long brown curls poking out from beneath his helmet.

"Hey mom, who's that?" A child called out loudly from behind me.

"I don't know, hon. Some kind of church person, I guess. Let's take her picture."

"*Bongiorno*," I repeated, overtop of the hubub. "I'm here to see Signora Fiuricii." I flashed the piece of Vatican stationery in front of his face.

"*Scusi. Parle italiano? Si?*" His face was really quite sweet, with a confused, puppy dog expression.

Good. He was confused. That was better than an outright refusal and a one-way ticket out of the Vatican.

"No. I don't speak Italiano. Ennggglisshhh."

"Inglish?" he repeated. "No inglish. *Deutsch*? *Français*?"

With my fingers crossed behind my back, I shook my head no. "No. Sorry, I speak English. I'm here to see this Signora. May I go through?" I began to inch towards the gate.

His baby brow furrowed in frustration, he motioned for my paper. The Vatican crest of the stationery received intense scrutiny, as did the name on the paper. "Fiuricii," he repeated slowly. "Fiuricii."

A priest came up behind me and glanced over my shoulder to see what was keeping us. He fidgeted with his watch, causing the guard to glance up.

"*Scusi, Padre. Uno momento.*" He gazed back down at the paper and began to mumble to himself in Italian.

The American child's voice piped up. "Mom, look, they're having a line-up to get in there."

"Just like Saturday at the Wal-Mart, isn't it, sweetums?"

The priest coughed behind me. The guard stared with greater concentration at the paper. I felt a trickle of sweat begin to slide its cool way down my back.

"May I go in now, please?" I urged.

I pointed in the direction of the gate and the guard thrust my paper back at me. "*Si, si, avante*," he said brusquely and waved me through.

I couldn't believe it. I was finally in.

It was as if I had stepped into another time. A narrow cobblestone road, shaded by the high walls of St. Peters, wound in front of me like something from a fifteenth-century Italian village. Where there had been the croaking background of tourist tongues, suddenly there was peace. Where there had been sunlight and heat in the open square, there was shade and cool. I slowly walked forward, drinking in the illicit childlike pleasure of being where I wasn't supposed to be.

I took a slurp of my almost forgotten gelato and glanced down at the map the nun had given me. It apeared that I had entered through the Arch of the Bells and was now walking across the Square of the First Roman Martyrs. The quiet piazza turned sharply to the left, a narrow lane running past the Teutonic College and the Sacristy of St. Peters. In front of me in the distance, I could see gardens. There was a haze of green, some palm trees, and the whirr of leaves brushing up against one another. A nun scuttled by me, and I let her pass. I wanted to be alone, to experience this secret Vatican all by myself.

"*Signora*!"

I rounded the corner and was brought up sharply by the sound of a man's voice. A security guard, not a Swiss one, brought me abruptly back to the twentieth century.

"*Bongiorno*," I sighed and once again flashed my piece of stationery.

This guard had a little cubicle and a telephone. There was a hurried phone conversation. "She no there," he said and pointed me in the direction of the press office. "Go there and try. *Prego*."

I took back my precious piece of paper and turned in the direction he had indicated. It was pointless, as I knew Signora Fiuricii wasn't going to be there, but I felt I must go through the motions if only for the sake of authenticity.

The press office was empty except for a receptionist and a cleaning lady. The cleaning lady spoke better English than the receptionist. After much discussion and telephoning, I was told the unsurprising fact that Signora Fiuricii was not in. Nor was anyone else I could speak to. Didn't I know that everyone was gone for the month of August? Rome was *caldo*.

I nodded my head wearily and left the building. Yes, Rome was *caldo*. Nobody was anywhere to be found in Italy, except perhaps on a stretch of sandy beach on Capri. Hell, even the Pope had vacated the city for the cooler climes of his summer retreat at Castel Gandolfo. Or had he? Was it possible that he was in residence right now? A white figure wandering through these ancient terra-cotta-coloured buildings? Perhaps even watching this unexpected and illegal visitor in the Square of the First Roman Martyrs?

With the watchful eye of the guard upon me, I raised my melone gelato in a silent salute. Here's to you, Pope John Paul II. A final slurp and it was gone, the cool melon flavour sliding down my throat. Laughing quietly to myself, I licked my fingers, refolded my map, and reentered St. Peters Square.

It was a short visit to the real Vatican, but still worth it. Tom would, after all, be proud of me. I had managed to get into the Vatican. I had not gotten in trouble. And I had shared my gelato with the Pope.

Tom and I decided to celebrate my victorious, if short, entry into the Vatican with a romantic dinner. The walk to the restaurant was peaceful after such a hectic day, the air cooling with the dusk. The landmarks of Rome's history rose up against the setting sun, like fantastic Gothic statuary. Ancient shrines led us in silhouetted grandeur down the streets of Rome, away from the Coliseum towards the Campo dei Fiori.

Our restaurant, one of the few left open, was crowded. Luckily, we got a table on the piazza. Tom held my hand as we ordered wine and pasta, his baby finger tickling my palm.

"We need an accordian player," he joked.

I laughed and took a sip of my wine. "An accordion player? What and some man singing '*O Solo Mio*'?"

Tom squinted his eyes again into his Mastroianni look and nodded his head in mock seriousness. "Definitely. This is an evening meant for romance."

The waiter scuttled up to our table, two flat serving dishes of smoky-flavoured spaghetti carbonara stretched along one arm.

"*Grazie*," I said as the steaming plate was placed in front of me.

As we dug into our meal, I noticed two carabiniere wander into the piazza. Bodies trim and muscular, uniforms like that of some Ruritarian colonel, they paused in front of the restaurant as if for effect.

"I think they're in love with each other," Tom said through a mouthful of spaghetti as he turned to look.

"I think they're in love with themselves."

They had that narcissistic look. Straight backs, caressingly tight pants, firm buttocks - a surprisingly homoerotic style from a society that proclaims its machismo so strongly.

The owner of the restaurant strolled out from the kitchen, a dirty napkin draped loosely around his waist, and waved to the two carabiniere. The tipping of his hand to his mouth suggested that they were welcome to come in for an aperitif.

The carabiniere conferred in an undertone, their bodies still sculpturally posed for our benefit, and then nodded their acceptance. They walked into the restaurant as if they owned it. I got a bored glance as they passed our table. Tom garnered a few seconds more.

"They like you," I teased.

Tom shrugged his shoulders. "I told you it was an evening meant for romance."

The carabiniere had been ensconced inside with their Sambucca for about five minutes when the alarm went off, a loud, pervasive clanging blaring out from one of the stores on the piazza. Most of the patrons of the restaurant put down their forks and gazed curiously out into the square, looking for any sign of burglars. Tom and I turned towards the entrance to the restaurant, awaiting the speedy departure of the defenders of Rome, the carabiniere.

No one appeared, except for our waiter, who was carrying a platter filled with dishes and looking harassed.

"They're not coming," Tom finally said.

"I realized that," I answered and swiveled towards the square. There was no movement, of either criminals or carabiniere. "Maybe it's a false alarm."

"Maybe," Tom said doubtfully.

We returned to our dinner. The alarm, a high pitched drone, continued as musical accompaniment. Finally, as we reached for our after dinner cappuccino, it stopped with an abrupt hiss. Silence settled over the piazza, except for the tinkling of cutlery against plates.

The carabiniere, as if unaware of any possible crime in progress, reappeared in the doorway and posed once again with a kind of fascist grace. They walked out into the piazza, paused, looked for any disturbance to the general peace, and finding nothing, strolled off in search of further Sambucca.

"Well, that's it. That's Rome in a nutshell," said Tom. "The easy life."

I smiled and shook my head. "No. Not quite the easy life. *La Dolce Vita*."

xv if it's lunch, this must be McDonald's ❖

Why not try a McDonald's in every country in Europe?

It was Tom's idea. He threw it out to me one day while we had been travelling through the French countryside. Eat at McDonald's? All over Europe? I could be excused for thinking this rather ridiculous, especially as we were surrounded by the bounty of French cuisine. No, no, no, he insisted. It was a weird thing to do, fun, the kind of thing you could talk about on Jeopardy.

Jeopardy?

Yes, he continued, Jeopardy. Everyone had some quirk or hobby that they discussed when they were guests on this American game show. His would be that he had eaten at a McDonald's in every country in Europe. Tom had, up until this point, kept hidden this secret desire to swap witty comments with Jeopardy host, Alex Trebek, and yell out things like "Historical figures for 100.".

Do you mean we'll collect McDonald's in the way that some people collect t-shirts or matchboxes? I replied

Exactly.

Tom had already tasted a Big Mac in Oxford Circus, french fries in Edinburgh and a Quarter Pounder in Dublin, so he was safe on that account. As I was not intending on unburdening myself to Alex Trebek, I would merely follow like a faithful adjutant, paper napkins and Alka Seltzer at the ready.

We kept up with Tom's new hobby all the way across the Continent. There were *ensaladas verdes* in the Puerto del Sol in Madrid and fresh apple juice in downtown Brussels. Mayonnaise topped our french fries in Amsterdam and there was a kind of McChicken in Norway. We continued to try local delicacies as well as picnicking with our own supplies. Sometimes we just managed to rush in to a McDonald's to fulfill our quota of one item before our train departed a country.

In Munich, that meant McBeer in plastic cups, and in Rome, it was cappuccino a la Mickey D's. Salzburg's McDonald's was located in the old part of the city, the architecture fitting in remarkably well with the surrounding buildings. And near Rome's Spanish Steps, we found the best-looking McDonald's yet, with waterfalls and brickwork that made it seem much more like a restaurant than a fast food joint.

Switzerland's, however, was the best. We stopped a young man outside the train station in Zurich when we were unable to spot the golden arches.

"Excuse me," I asked, "Do you have a McDonald's here?"

He was a student, a bag of books hung over the bar of his bicycle. "You want to eat at McDonald's?" He smiled and shook his head. "But we have such wonderful food here - raclette, fondue, chocolate - why do you want to come to Switzerland and eat that stuff?"

I blushed, agreeing with what him but unable to explain our weird hobby. "It's difficult to explain. You do have a McDonald's here?" I pressed on.

He sighed and pointed down the street. "Yes. Down there about five blocks."

I nodded my thanks and he biked away, disgusted with our unsophisticated palates.

After all that embarrassment, we found Zurich to have the most expensive McDonald's so far, as well as the best food. Our amateur survey ranked their milkshakes top of the list, with a rich creamy chocolateness.

Definitely two thumbs up.

We traversed the capitals of Europe like two bloodhounds following a trail of empty Big Mac boxes. Finally, we arrived in Greece. In Constitution Square in Athens, Tom stopped a young businesswoman for directions.

"Could you tell me where I can find a McDonald's?"

"McDonald's?" She smiled, the whiteness of her teeth contrasting with the attractive olive tan of her skin. "I'm afraid we don't have any McDonald's in Greece."

She walked away, leaving Tom and I standing stunned on the sidewalk.

"No McDonald's," Tom whispered. "All this trouble, all those hamburgers. We won't be able to say we ate at a McDonald's in every country we visited. What am I going to tell Alex?"

"It's all right, sweetie," I said, comforting him with an arm around his shoulder, "you'll think of something else to tell him."

It took several stiff ouzos to help Tom over the loss.

***

Food was both a constant worry and a fascination for us during the trip. There were even times when, facing stratospheric costs, we wondered whether we could actually afford to eat. Eating in good restaurants was a treat we saved for special occasions.

We ate most of our meals in small, inexpensive restaurants or picknicked with fresh produce from local markets. There were sliced tomato and cucumber salads, drizzled with a wonderful *fines herbes* dressing I picked up in Paris. Fresh bread could be bought cheaply everywhere. We picked up fragrant herbed salamis in German markets or *mortadella* and *fromaggio* on crusty buns in Roman delicatessens. A bottle of wine chilled in the bathroom sink, or perhaps a few bottles of Amstel floating prettily in the bath, and we had as good a beverage as any restaurant could offer. An after dinner stroll and maybe a splurge for a coffee or ice cream, and we were happy.

In Greece, however, we splurged. The food was inexpensive and plentiful; and, because it was the end of our trip, we ate out more frequently. On our first night in Athens, we found a nearly empty taverna near our hotel.

"Tzatziki to start and then the moussaka, please," I told the waiter.

He bobbed his head in smiling agreement and turned his attention to Tom. "And you, sir?"

"I think I'll try the squid. And some retsina to drink, please." Tom's eyes wandered over the tabletop. "Do you have butter here? For the bread?"

The waiter straightened himself up, his lips sliding off his teeth in offense. "Of course we have butter, sir. This is Athens, after all. What do you think we would have?" Bristling, he picked up Tom's menu and trotted off to the kitchen.

I took a sip of my mineral water. "You've offended him, Tom."

"I don't know why. All I did was ask if they had any butter for my bread. I wasn't trying to insinuate that they were a backward country and didn't know what butter was."

A few minutes later, the owner scuttled up to our table, proffering a white saucer on which were placed two tiny pats of butter.

"Here you are, sir. Your elephant butter."

We could hear giggling from behind the closed kitchen door.

Tom's eyebrows lifted. "Elephant butter?"

"Yes. You asked whether we have butter here. In Greece, we get our butter from elephants."

"I see."

I smiled into my tzatziki and tried not to laugh.

Tom took a knifeful of butter and spread it thinly over a piece of bread. "It's fine, thank you."

With a knowing smile, the owner retreated to the laughter in the kitchen.

"So how is it, really? The elephant butter?" I asked.

Tom pointed the sticky knife at me. "Now don't you start."

I started to laugh. "Is it pungent, you know, a kind of wild, gamey taste? Does it have a BIG flavour?"

"Shut up and eat your tzatziki."

The moussaka and squid arrived a short while later. The plates were silently placed in front of us. I waited for the inevitable comment about the butter.

"Enjoy your meal," the waiter said and then smiled over at Tom. "Your elephant butter, sir, it is to your satisfaction?"

Tom was trying to be a good sport about it, but the joke was beginning to wear a bit thin. "Yes, fine," he answered through gritted teeth.

"Good." A bow and he disappeared.

There was a surprising amount of activity in that restaurant, especially considering that we were the only patrons. It seemed that every few minutes a waiter or bus boy would wander by and make some comment about the butter.

"Did you like your elephant butter, sir?" the bus boy asked with a grin as he removed our plates. "I could get you some more, if you would like it?"

Tom fixed him with a steely glare and said nothing.

Our original waiter swept up to our table, proffering the dessert menu. "Would you care for some dessert now?"

Before I could say anything, Tom had pushed his seat back and stood up. "I'm afraid not. All that elephant butter, you see, has filled me up." Tom tossed down a few bills and grabbed me by the elbow, steering me out of the restaurant.

"But Tom, I wanted some baklava."

"You can get baklava at another restaurant." His jaw was set firmly.

I couldn't resist. "But why, Tom? Didn't you like your elephant butter?"

***

I think we had the best meal of the trip on a ferry in the middle of the Adriatic Sea.

It was the mid-afternoon of a gorgeous autumn day. We sat alone on the deserted deck of a chugging Italian ferry that was taking us from the island of Corfu to Patras, on the Greek mainland. The Adriatic was stretched like a taut band of blue silk in front us, hardly a ripple on its heat-seared surface. Pop music serenaded us from tinny speakers while we sipped cheap red wine from plastic cups.

I sliced open a loaf of bread and layered in some butter and goat cheese for Tom. The heat played like dappled notes through the metal awning on my face. I took a bite of the bread and then followed it with a sip of wine, feeling the strong cheese wash down my throat. Flaky apple pastries, triangular and sticky sweet, dusted our laps with crumbs.

We chewed, eyes closed, half asleep. I felt drugged with the heat and the wine and the warmth of Tom's arm around me. A perfect afternoon.

"May I have this dance?" Tom whispered in my ear.

I stood up and he enfolded me in his arms. We moved slowly to the music, Tom in his battered jeans and a tank top, me in a pair of khaki shorts and a t-shirt. Our bags, like the bundled belongings of refugees, were huddled around us on the deck, outlining the boundaries of our dance floor.

A deckhand walked by. He did not seem to mind the two tourists rocking gently in one another's arms, oblivious to everyone, an empty wine bottle rolling slowly along the length of the deck.

The music stopped. But we kept on dancing.

xvi a day with the Athens police ❖❖❖❖

It is like this," the tall, horse-faced policewoman started, "we need to know where you were robbed."

I sighed and looked up at a fly that was dodging an aging ceiling fan. "And what if I don't know where I was robbed?"

The policewoman gave a weary sigh. I was, it appeared, going to be difficult.

I turned to look at Tom, who, wilting from the baking Athenian heat, had slumped onto a wooden seat. He was staring into space, having given up on listening to my cross-examination by the policewoman.

I knew how he was feeling.

It had started out as a peaceful day of sightseeing. We were in Athens for a few days before heading out to the islands where I was to write the last installment of my column. What is the first place one visits in Athens? The Acropolis, of course.

Scrambling like goats over the loose stones, we visited the ancient sun-washed temples. In the wonderful heat, my hair bleaching blonde from the sun, my limbs tanned and strong from weeks of wandering around the Mediterranean, I felt rather god-like and invincible myself.

That was my first mistake.

I passed on visiting the Museum of Anthropology with Tom after lunch. No more museums for me, please, I wanted nothing more than a nice heat-drugged nap. I would walk home alone.

Second mistake, right there.

I am sure I had my camera as I left the Plaka area of Athens, but somewhere between there and my hotel room a light-fingered thief had separated me from my beloved Nikon.

I think it was in Omonia Square. These two men jumped in front of me and began to scream at me in Greek. Then they dashed away. But I'm really not sure. I carry my knapsack on that shoulder and so I didn't know when the camera was cut away."

A light of hope lit up the policewoman's equine features. "Omonia Square. You did say Omonia Square?"

"Yes," I started out, "but I'm really not sure ..."

A thick, olive-skinned hand shot out firmly in mid-air to stop my meandering. "We say Omonia Square. No, no," she cut off my protests. "You realize that you will not get your camera back?"

With a gulp, I nodded my head yes. I might be ridiculously honest, but I wasn't a fool.

"Good. Most tourists do not understand that they will never get their belongings back. Now, we have to have a location for the crime. You were robbed in Omonia Square, alright?"

With a guilty nod, I agreed. Tom, I noticed, was smiling to himself.

"For this, you must go to the police station in Omonia Square."

"Can't you handle it here?"

Once again those almond-shaped, hazel eyes settled with irritation upon my face. "We are the Tourist Police here," she answered, as if that were explanation enough. "It is on Nikias Street. I will give you a map." She spread a map out across the counter and pinpointed the street.

I nudged Tom to stand up. "Wake up. We've got another police station to visit."

Tom glanced at his watch. "You said this morning that we'd be through by lunchtime."

"I know, but I've got to get this police report or my insurance company won't replace the camera. We should be finished by one," I said as we headed back out onto the street. "After all, how long can it take to get a police report?"

Mistake number three.

Omonia. Ooomonia Square," the policeman drawled out the *O* as if he had an egg in his mouth. "Oomonia Square. Yyyyeeees."

We were in the Omonia Square police station. It had been a long, hot walk from the Tourist Police office downtown, and an even warmer wait to speak to this police officer, whose lack of English skills made our previous policewoman seem heavenly by comparison. He was red-headed, a change from the dark colouring of the Greeks, with a moustache that he wiggled when he was thinking.

"Yes, that's right. She was robbed in Omonia Square," Tom cut in in an effort to hurry things along a bit. It was already twelve thirty, and we had a boat to catch to Crete that evening.

"Well, I'm not sure about the location ..." I started out, my words withering under Tom's angry gaze.

"She was robbed in Omonia Square. Okay? Could you give us the report now, PLEASE," Tom continued.

The policeman's moustache wiggled. His brown eyes bobbed from Tom's face to my own, like tiny dark ping-pong balls, but he said nothing.

"I was on my way to our hotel by the train station when they jumped in front of me and took the camera," I offered.

The police officer looked up hopefully. "Train?"

"Well, yes, by the train station, that's where our hotel is."

"Train, yes? Stolen. Train." He seemed quite pleased at this revelation. He quickly scrawled a note on a piece of paper. Speaking to Tom, who he seemed to feel was in charge of the situation, he tapped one finger at the note. "Go Theodorious Street."

"What do you mean 'Go Theodorious Street'? Is that another police station?"

"Police? Yes."

"But we're already with the police, though God knows, I'm beginning to wonder!" Tom sputtered angrily.

The police officer sat back in his seat, offended.

"Look, you are our second police station today," I inserted calmly. "All we want is a police report for a stolen item. Can't you give that to us?"

The police officer, who looked as if he hadn't understood a word I had just said, merely tapped briskly at the note and then walked out of the room in a huff.

We had no alternative. It was onto police station number three.

Tom sat silently in the cab as it whizzed us with an agility that defied the basic laws of physics through traffic. His jaw was clenched tight, a sure sign that trouble was on the horizon.

"I'm sorry about all this, Tom."

"It's not your fault," he said shortly, continuing to stare out the window.

"Well, I know it isn't, but still it was *my* camera ..."

"I said, it's NOT YOUR FAULT, okay?"

I sat back in my seat, stung by the harshness of his tone.

Great, that was all we needed right now, a fight.

The taxi disgorged us in front of 23 Theodorious Street. It was obviously more important than the Omonia Square station. This seven storey building had its own patch of grass and a sputtering water fountain. The guard, a young soldier in a pressed uniform, pointed a menacing uzi at us as we approached the front door.

The lobby was large, cool and curiously empty. The slippery green marble accentuated the desolation of the place, its only inhabitant a security officer standing in an alcove. We crossed the expanse of the lobby and presented him with our note from the officer at the Omonia Square station.

The guard was a heavy man, almost circular around the waistline, crammed into a tight beige uniform. "You have been robbed?" he asked me, his black, doe-like eyes settling on my face.

I nodded my head yes.

"You come at a bad time to see police."

I glanced at my watch and sighed. Was there ever a good time?

"Bad time? It's only two o'clock. Are they still eating lunch?"

The security officer waggled his head in a non-commital fashion. "No. They're not here."

"What do you mean, not here?" Tom interjected with a note of simmering anger in his voice.

The security officer waved his hand towards the deserted lobby, as if that were explanation enough.

"When will *they* be in?" I asked.

"An hour?" He sounded unsure. "You come back later?"

"No, we're not going to come back later!" Tom shouted angrily. "We're going to stay right here until someone looks after us!"

"Yes," I agreed. "We're not moving until we get some help!"

A few minutes later we found ourselves back outside, simmering in the hot afternoon sun.

"Well, at least he said we could come back in in an hour," I offered in an attempt to bolster my wounded pride.

Tom said nothing. He was having a glowering contest with the soldier with the uzi.

"Fine. Don't talk to me. Just sit and sulk. I'll go and see if something can actually be DONE."

And with that I left the two of them attempting to out-stare one another and headed off to find a payphone.

I found one in a magazine kiosk a block away. The kiosk was typically Athenian, a wooden booth plunked out on the middle of the sidewalk. It sold everything from food to drinks to pornographic postcards. The phone, an elderly black one, sat on a stool with its telephone cord trailing back across the sidewalk and into another building. I handed the aged newsagent a few drachma and began to hunt down the number of the Canadian Embassy.

A few soft rings and then the annoying tone of an answering machine. "I'm sorry, but the Canadian Embassy is closed. Thank you for calling, and please try again during our regular office hours."

I slammed the receiver down with a vehemence that shocked the newsagent from his contemplation of a newspaper. "Sorry about that. They're not in, you see."

He examined the condition of the receiver before going back to his reading.

I tried again, this time the British Embassy.

"Thank you for calling the Embassy of the United Kingdom. I am sorry, but our office is closed for the day."

"DAMMIT!"

The newsagent's face appeared over the top of page one and then disappeared again.

I finally got a real, live human voice to answer the phone at the American Embassy. To my inquiry of how to get a police report for a stolen camera in Athens, I received a pleasant but weary reply.

"I have no idea where you should go, ma'am. I'm sorry, but it's very difficult to get anything done here. Things in Greece don't work the way they do back home."

I didn't bother to explain that my home was a little bit north of her own. I understood what she meant.

The hour had all but passed by the time I arrived back at 23 Theodorious Street. Tom and the soldier appeared to have called it a draw and were now staring at other things. I handed Tom a wedge of orange as a peace offering, which he accepted with a grumble.

"Shall we try again inside?"

"Sure."

The security officer watched our entry into the lobby with obvious displeasure. "Nobody here!" he called out.

"Look, there's got to be someone. It's the middle of the afternoon," I said. "Could you check for us? Please?"

I'm not sure whether it was a desire to rid himself of these bothersome tourists or my spaniel-like eye watering, but he threw his hands up in resignation and picked up the phone. After a lengthy conversation, he gathered up two clip-on identification badges. "Stavros will come and get you," he supplied and handed them to us.

Stavros, when he arrived, was pleasant but not particularly helpful, mainly because he couldn't speak a word of English. He deposited Tom and I in an empty office and then disappeared.

Tom made himself comfortable on a couch that looked like it had survived intact from the sixties, while I went to investigate our new surroundings. The entire floor was empty. The only sign of life was a couple of street cops drinking coffee in one room.

"I can't find anyone," I told Tom when I returned. "I mean, no one. It's like a morgue in here."

"It looks like it, too."

Tom was right. I glanced around the walls of the sunlit office at the faded photographs of people in severe sixties suits. It was as if the room and its furnishings had somehow been held suspended in time for the past three decades. No multi-line phone-faxes here. A single black rotary phone, much like the newsagent's, sat quietly on a desktop.

The clicking of heels on the linoleum corridor heralded the return of Stavros. With a smile and a wave of one hand, he prodded us forward and into the elevator again. Up to another floor and down numerous empty hallways until he guided us into another room.

There was a middle-aged man waiting for us there, seated behind a desk in a large corner office. We guessed from Stavros's deferential air that he was important. A chief detective, perhaps.

Stavros pointed us towards two seats in the outer waiting room, but I stepped past him and up to the chief detective's desk. Stavros' olive skin lightened a shade or two, his ingratiating smile slipping downward.

Tom coughed nervously into his hand. "I think maybe we should just wait out here, Kim."

I ignored Tom. To hell with politeness. I was going to get something done here.

"Hello. I'm sorry, I mean *Kalimera*."

The chief detective, whose expression had stiffened with irritation upon my impolite entry, relaxed into a pleasant smile. "*Kalimera*."

"I'm here because I was robbed yesterday. Of my camera. In Omonia Square." I paused and waited for some reaction. There was none. "I would like a police report, please."

He shook his head and murmured something in Greek. He was holding the note from the Omonia Square station in his hand.

"Can you speak English?" There was no comprehension on his face. "*Deutsch? Français? Italiano?*" I hurried on, throwing out languages as if I was a U.N. translator.

"*Italiano*?" He perked up a bit at this.

"No, sorry. Got a bit carried away there. I can't speak Italian. But I do need a report."

He shook his head slowly, uncomprehending.

"My camera." I made a clicking gesture with my forefinger on a phantom camera. "Gone." I pantomimed a hand ripping it off my shoulder. "I need a report now." He watched intently as I wrote on an imaginary piece of paper. "We catch a boat from Piraeus at seven o'clock." I pointed to the seven on his wall clock.

"Yesssss," he said finally. His voice was quite lovely, thick and dark like Greek coffee. "Yes."

I had done it! He was beginning to understand me.

He pointed to the seven on the clock and then began to wave me out of the office.

"Goodbye," Stavros said from behind me and then, to prove that he was multilingual added, "*Ciao*."

"Whhatt?" I sputtered out. "I'm not going anywhere."

I heard a weary sigh come from the outer room. It was Tom. "He thinks you're telling him that we'll come back at seven this evening."

"No, no. We're supposed to take a boat at seven o'clock," I insisted hurriedly. There was another pantomime of a boat on the waves. "Piraeus. Seven o'clock."

The chief detective's face fell. He had understood that. He said something in Greek to Stavros, who pushed me out into the waiting room and closed the door behind them.

There was a murmured discussion between the two that was followed by much telephoning. Thirty minutes later, Stavros reappeared. He smiled at us and pointed to the door, nodding his head happily.

A policewoman in a stylish lime green linen dress soon arrived. She stepped up to me and held out her hand. "*Bonjour. Parlez-vous français*?"

It is not too much to say that Tom had to stop me from throwing myself gratefully at her feet. I explained in semi-bad French what had happened. Stavros handed her the note from the Omonia Square station.

"You say you were robbed in Omonia Square?" she asked in French.

"Yes."

"This note says that you were robbed on the train coming into Athens."

My mind flashed back to the previous policeman's hopeful repetition of the word train, and my heart sank. "No, I was robbed near my hotel which is by the *train station*."

The policewoman translated this to Stavros and the chief. There was much rolling of eyes and waving of hands. The policewoman wrote something on the bottom of the note and handed it back to me.

"You have been sent to the wrong police station. Here we handle national crimes, such as those that occur while in transit on the train. You will have to return to the Omonia Square station."

"You're kidding."

The policewoman, who had been crisply businesslike, allowed herself a small smile. "The chief detective is calling there now for you. They will be alerted that you will be arriving soon, and should be prepared for you. I have also written it down for them on the note."

The taxi ride back to Omonia Square was conducted in silence. We screeched to a stop in front of the station, and I was out the door and charging towards the police guard before Tom could even move.

"Stop!" the guard commanded sharply as I headed up the cracked cement steps towards him.

"Get out of my bloody way!" I pushed the muzzle of the uzi out of my path and continued at a run up the narrow stairway.

"Kim! What the hell are you doing!" Tom called from behind me. I could hear shouting in Greek and English, as both Tom and the guard raced up the stairs after me.

I sprinted around the corner, through a crowded room - I remember a group of street cops looking up in shock as this red-headed woman stormed through their office - and then I was through the door and into the same office I had entered five hours previously. I skidded to a stop, the guard and Tom stumbling in behind me.

The red-headed police officer, whose initial mistake had caused this horrible day, was in the process of handcuffing an Italian drug dealer. The dealer, who was sprawled face down on a desk over his drug paraphernalia, looked up with interest at my sudden entrance. I'm sure he thought the mafia was coming to save him.

There was a shout of Greek from the police officer at the group of us, followed by an equally loud blast of Italian at the drug dealer. He picked the handcuffed criminal up off the desk and thrust him across the room into the care of the guard. Turning to us, he pointed to some chairs in the opposite corner.

"I... want... my... report," I said, slowly and precisely. The shock of stumbling in on this arrest had taken some of the wind out of my sails.

The police officer sat down heavily in his chair and let out a stream of incomprehensible words that no doubt cast aspersions on my parenthood

"Listen, all I want is a bloody police report."

He answered in Greek, picking up a piece of paper and flapping it in the air.

"Just give me the damn report. I can't understand a word you're saying!"

"*Kapnopoli? Tsigaro?*" He picked up a pen and scribbled artistically on a piece of paper. "*Stylo. Papier.*"

"Pen and paper," Tom translated.

"Yes," I answered, "We got that last bit. *Vous parlez français*?"

"*Ohi.*" His Greek *no* was snorted out in disgust. He sat closer to me, as if his proximity might somehow improve my comprehension. "Tabacchi?"

"Tabacchi? What the hell is tabacchi?"

"Tabacchi, tabacchi!!" His fair skin had mottled into a crimson hue, and he was banging his fists with frustration on the desktop. He slammed his chair back against the wall and called out a name.

A young officer of about twenty-two came into the office. There was a murmured discussion before the young cop sidled up to me.

"*Tsigaro*? Tabacchi?" he asked persuasively, pointing towards the door.

I was getting sick of this tabacchi business. "I don't know what you're talking about!"

With a roughness that was more due to inexperience than actual intent, the young officer grabbed me by the upper arm and yanked me out of my seat. "Tabacchi!" he shouted and began to pull me towards the door.

"What are you doing? Where are you taking her?" Tom shot out of his chair and started after us. There was a scuffle as the red-headed officer attempted to restrain him.

"It's alright, Tom. I can take care of myself," I called back like a romantic heroine headed for the guillotine.

"Kim!"

I craned my head back and saw the police officer forcing Tom's head to the ground.

And then I was dragged out the door and through the station room and down the winding, smelly staircase. But rather than being pulled into some darkened interrogation room, I was pulled past the security guard and out into the street.

"Tabacchi," the young officer said again, and pointed with his free hand across the street.

There, tucked into a tiny cubbyhole off the pathway, was a tiny tobacconists shop, or as they said in a garbled attempt at English, tabacchi.

"I get it. The tabacchi," I said, comprehension dawning.

The officer pulled me through the streaming traffic and up to an elderly man who sat surrounded by newspapers and sun-bleached packages of Marlboros. The officer released my arm, leaving a pattern of pink welts. He explained something to the tobacconist, who disappeared like a gnome behind the counter. He reappeared holding a number of forms and placed them down in front of me.

"Drachma," the young officer said, pointing at the forms.

I gazed down at the official-looking papers. I looked up at the officer who was now pointing at my bag, and began to laugh. "They're my police report. You want me to buy my police report forms from the tobacconist". I pulled out my wallet and, still laughing, doled out the coins to the tobacconist.

His job done, the officer allowed me to find my own way back to the station.

Kim, are you alright?"

I was met at the door of the office by a distraught Tom. I gave him a hug, still laughing to myself. "Everything's fine. They were just trying to get me to go and buy the police report form, that's all."

"Go and buy the police report?"

"Yes, that's right. From the tobacconist across the road." I waved the papers in front of me. "You see, tabacchi. That's what they were getting at."

I stepped past a stupefied Tom and placed the forms on the desk in front of the officer. He managed a wintry smile, rubbing one wrist which appeared to have suffered somewhat from his battle with Tom. He picked up the phone, spoke to someone for a moment, and then wordlessly handed it to me.

"Hello?" I said into the receiver.

"Hello? This is the Tourist Police," a male voice said. "I am going to translate for you with Officer Stephanopolous. First, I need the name of your camera and all other descriptions of the crime."

I listed all the information I had about the camera, the place that I believed it was stolen and the two men who had stolen it.

"Yes, yes," the voice said briskly. "Now, this camera was stolen with violence, was it not?"

"No, I wouldn't say so. Not with violence."

There was a hiss of frustration on the other end of the line. "No, no, no. You do not understand me. This camera was stolen with violence."

"No, really, it wasn't ..."

"Listen, THIS CAMERA WAS STOLEN WITH VIOLENCE!"

I paused, remembering our first policewoman of the day and the convoluted path that sticking to the truth had taken me.

"Okay, my camera was stolen with violence," I repeated and was rewarded with a relieved sigh from the tourist policeman.

I looked at my watch. It was five fifteen. It had taken me almost eight hours and an entire day with the Athens police, but I was finally getting the hang of Greek justice.

xvii going home ❖❖❖❖❖❖❖❖❖❖❖

If this were the end of a romantic movie, perhaps starring Cary Grant and some beautiful starlet, Tom would be holding my hand while I cried into a tall, cool drink. The Aegean would be lapping gently beside us while a bouzouki band played softly in the background.

I looked down at the dripping can of Coca-Cola resting between my feet. The Aegean was not lapping placidly beside me, it was crashing with wind driven force into the seawall, and Tom was not holding my hand. He was holding the back of my neck while I placed my head between my knees and tried not to throw up.

"I'm alright."

"Are you sure? Do you want me to take you to the restaurant over there? I'm sure they'd let you use their washroom, especially if you look like you're about to throw up in the middle of their dining room."

I sniffled pitifully. I was beginning to cry, although not in the romantic, non-mascara-running way I had hoped for.

"No, I think it's passed. I'll just take another sip of this flat Coke and see if it helps any."

Tom handed me a piece of dry melba toast from a crumpled package, and I took a half-hearted nibble.

Everything had been fine up until the previous evening. We had arrived in Crete, after our disasterous day with the Athenian Police, and had rented a moped to tour the island's archaeological sites. The sun was out, the food wonderful and inexpensive, and the water an Aegean aquamarine.

Santorini was jaggedly volcanic and fascinating. For the first time on this five-month odyssey, I gave myself up to the pleasure of a real holiday. We splashed in the ocean and then stripped off our salty suits and lay flecked with white sand on an isolated beach. It was September and Greece was a peaceful paradise.

Our next was Paros, my last island before I was due to return to Athens and then fly on to New York. The sunlit days were now tinged with sadness. I would be returning to Canada a week earlier than Tom. For the first time in months, we would be saying goodbye. Not just to this adventure that had brought us together, but also to one another.

It was the last full day we would have together. We bussed to the jetty for the small, rusty ferry across to Antiparos, an isolated sister island. It was the best way to remember Greece. White houses tumbling into the sea, a circular harbour with a few fishing boats bobbing in it. A lonely dog, not more than a puppy, was stretched out by the waterfront tavernas, awaiting someone to sit down for a glass of ouzo, a game of backgammon, and a pat.

We skirted the rutted, dusty roads to find small, empty beaches lapped by the Aegean. We took a bus up to the caves, dark and dripping stalagmites, and studied the ancient graffiti of earlier travellers, some carved as long ago as the French Revolution.

The main street of the island was all but deserted. We entered an empty restaurant, intrigued by the promise of a garden. Through the darkened interior, we found a back garden rich with flowers and fluttering butterflies. We ate from glass goblets filled with thick Greek yogurt drizzled with syrup-like honey and wrote final postcards home. We kissed beneath the hanging flower baskets and reminisced about our trip together.

That evening we went out to the best restaurant in Paros for a romantic dinner. It was lovely, an outdoor patio lit with flickering gas lanterns. We really didn't need expensive food to make things special. We had had as many good meals in cheap tavernas, drinking Dutch beer and eating what Greeks call a country salad, thick wedges of tomatoes, peppers and cucumbers, drizzled with olive oil and liberally spattered with hunks of salty feta cheese and marble-like black olives.

We were half-way through our spicy stifados when I began to notice an uncomfortable feeling in my stomach. I tried to ignore it. After all, I wanted this night to be special. But by the time the coffee arrived, I knew that this was more than just a touch of tummy trouble. I was going to be sick.

I managed to get down a bit of my coffee, listening half-heartedly to what Tom was saying, before I touched him on the arm.

"I'm sorry, Tom, but we're going to have to go now."

"Go?" he said, his brow furrowing in surprise. "What's the matter? Is there something wrong with your coffee?"

I shook my head no and pushed my seat back. "I don't feel very well. I think we should start walking back to the hotel."

The firm tone of my voice must have convinced Tom of the impending reappearance of my dinner for he hurriedly paid the bill and then grabbed my arm and walked me out of the restaurant.

I remember some of the walk back to the hotel, the paper lanterns sending a hazy glow over the whitewashed buildings, the slow strolling of the after dinner pedestrians. I remember Tom occasionally leaning forward to get a better look at my face, which I suppose was getting greener by the minute, and then picking up speed towards the hotel.

I am proud to say I made it. To the hotel room, that is. No ignominious throwing up in the gutter of the main street like a drunken Brit. No. I got within a hundred feet of the hotel, key in hand, and broke into a desperate run for the bathroom. Five minutes later, all of that expensive food had disappeared into the Paros sewer system, and I felt immeasurably better.

I even, foolishly, thought it was over. Tom, who has more sense than I do at times, didn't think so. He dug up a book of mine and proceeded to make himself comfortable for a sleepless night.

He was right. I continued to be sick, over gradually lengthening intervals, for the next ten hours. It was horrible. The sickest I've ever been, except for one terrible bout of food poisoning when I was a teenager. Tom, like some bizarre Lamaze coach, kept track of the time between my vomiting as if they were contraction pains.

"You're doing better now. It's been almost forty-five minutes since you last threw up."

Somehow, as I was gagging into the toilet, that didn't offer much comfort.

Dawn arrived, and with it a weak pot of tea and lemon from the patroness of the hotel. Apparently I had kept everyone else up most of the night as well. I sipped at the tea, feeling like a lone survivor on a storm tossed ship. If I was careful and didn't move, I'd be alright.

I lay in that bed like a mummy for the next six hours. Tom went off into town in a valiant attempt to see if he could get my TWA ticket from Athens switched to a later date. No. Could they possibly get me on an Olympic Airways flight to Athens tonight, so that I wouldn't have to sit through five hours on the ferry? Not a seat available.

He arrived back in mid-afternoon, complete with flat Coke and melba toast, to tell me that the best he could offer was a ticket on the hydrofoil that night. At least it was more comfortable than the ferry and was a shorter trip. It also, he added, had a cleaner washroom.

Evening came, and with it the realization that I was somehow going to have to move. Tom packed my bags, dressed me in a pair of black pants and a t-shirt and then lifted me like a rag doll towards the door. It was no good. He was going to have to call a taxi.

With the help of the taxi driver, they got me into the back seat of the car and drove the five blocks to the pier.

I have no idea what I must have looked like to the group of posh gold sandaled holidaymakers gathering to board the new, expensive hydrofoil. Barely able to stand, drugged to the hilt with Dramamine, gripping a can of Coke like a life line, I sat down on a cement curb beside the water.

Tom paid the driver and retrieved my bags. "Are you going to make it?" he asked worriedly.

"Sure," I said, my words muffled by the fact that my head was between my knees and I was trying not to throw up again. "I'll be fine."

"You can just ditch your ticket, Kim. Take a later flight back to Canada."

"I can't throw away eight hundred dollars, Tom. If I'm still breathing, I'm going to be on that plane." I felt his hand gently brush against the back of my head. I lifted my sweaty face from my lap. "I'm sorry I ruined everything."

A teasing smile, the one that had drawn me to him all those months ago, spread across his face. He looked gentle and sweet, and I felt a hollow breathlessness in my chest.

"What do you mean, ruined everything? What's one night? It's not the end of the world."

I was sniffling now, which attracted the attention of the other passengers. "It's the end of our world though, isn't it?" I said, not caring how soppy I sounded.

Tom pulled me to him and kissed the top of my forehead, sticky and dusty as it was. "No, it isn't."

The hydrofoil roared up to the dock in an ear-splitting whir of air and water. A stewardess in a natty uniform jumped out and helped push a platform up to the entry area and motioned the assorted group of passengers to begin to board.

"What do you mean?" I shouted, but Tom was already picking up my bags with one hand and pulling me up with the other.

"C'mon, they're boarding," he shouted back.

We walked as quickly as I could manage to the door, the rest of the passengers having already boarded. Tears were trickling down my face, and my stomach was reacting to this sudden movement as if I was on a roller coaster. The stewardess took my ticket from Tom's hand and motioned me on.

"I've got to help her on. She's sick!" Tom shouted, trying to speak above the roar of the whirring motor.

The stewardess began to shake her head no, but then stopped when she saw my pale, tear-stained cheeks. "Yes, alright, but you must come off as soon as she is seated," she said. "We're running behind schedule and we must depart as soon as everyone is boarded."

Tom half-carried me on board, dropping my bags in the aisle and seating me in a front seat. Everyone on board the hydrofoil was staring at us. I didn't care. Tears were streaming down my face now, and it almost didn't matter that I felt like I was going to throw up again. Everything had gone wrong. Our last evening together destroyed. Our romantic goodbyes ruined. Nothing was as I would have liked it to be.

"Kim." I looked up into Tom's face, still wallowing in my misery. "Stop crying, Kim. I'm going to have to go in a minute."

I hiccuped to a stop, and breathed deeply to quieten myself.

One slim, tanned hand brushed against my face, taking with it a healthy coating of dust and salty tears. "You take care of yourself, okay?"

I nodded and felt his arms come around me in a tight hug. "I love you." His lips grazed my own. "I'll see you in a few weeks."

"What?" I sat up in my seat as he started away from me at a run down the aisle, the stewardess pointing with agitation towards the door.

"Didn't you know?" he called from the doorway, the same mischevious grin spread across his face. "I'm not going to let you go now!"

And he was gone out the door.

The passengers, bereft of half their entertainment, swiveled their heads to watch me.

I paused for a moment, smiled wetly, blissfully, joyfully, and then staggered to the bathroom to throw up.

About the Author

Kim Herdman is a travel writer and journalist. She is a graduate of the University of British Columbia with a degree in English Literature. She has worked in many fields, ranging from newspapers to television. Her travel exploits have been chronicled on CBC radio and in newspapers throughout North America.

She lives in Vancouver with her partner, Stuart, and the joy and bane of their existence, Annie the cat.

To order Gelato with the Pope:
and other adventures of a travel writer in Europe, *please contact your local bookstore or:*

Sandhill Book Marketing Ltd.
#99-1270 Ellis Street (rear)
Kelowna, British Columbia V1Y 1Z4
Phone: (250) 763-1406 Fax: (250) 763-4051
Order line: 1-800-667-3848